INSIDE KENSINGTON PALACE

When Diana arrives home the transformation is almost immediate. She will often literally kick off her shoes and skip down the entrance hall, before going up to her dressing room to change into a trendy outfit from her extensive private wardrobe. The days when she would arrive home and slump, totally drained, against the front door or sit silently in a chair, are now gone.

Staff smile at the image of her wearing matronly fashions. Her working clothes — when she worries about the wind, children looking up her skirt and flying the flag — are far removed from her private outfits. At home she wears slinky satin trousers, sexy leather skirts and sensual silk blouses. At the same time she is certainly a home maker who enjoys the simple pleasures of family life. But there is more to her than a one dimensional caricature of the winsome wife and mother.

About the Author

Andrew Morton has been a Fleet Street royal correspondent for the last six years and has travelled with members of the royal family on all their major foreign tours. He is a regular TV and radio commentator in Europe and North America and has written a number of books on the royal family including *Duchess*, the first full-length biography of the Duchess of York.

Andrew Morton lives in London with his wife and their two children.

Inside Kensington Palace

Andrew Morton

From D. & H. Toovey
to H. Crowther
1986

NEW ENGLISH LIBRARY
Hodder and Stoughton

Copyright © 1987 by Andrew Morton

First published in Great Britain in 1987
by Michael O'Mara Books Ltd

First New English Library Paperback
edition 1988

British Library C.I.P.

Morton, Andrew, *1953–*
    Inside Kensington Palace.
    1. London. Kensington and Chelsea
    (London Borough). Palaces:
    Kensington Palace. Royal families.
    Private life
    I. Title
941.085'8'0922

ISBN 0 450 43113 4

Printed and bound in Great Britain
for Hodder and Stoughton
Paperbacks, a division of Hodder and
Stoughton Ltd., Mill Road,
Dunton Green, Sevenoaks, Kent
TN13 2YA (Editorial Office:
47 Bedford Square, London
WC1B 3DP) by Cox & Wyman Ltd.,
Reading.

Contents

Acknowledgments

Question: 'What's the difference between Buckingham Palace and the Kremlin?'
Answer: 'About 2,000 miles.'

This cynical joke about the secrecy surrounding the royal family is sadly accurate. Our present royal family are more obsessed with their definition of privacy yet more conscious of promoting their image than at any time this century. It therefore makes the task of anyone trying to write a contemporary account of their lives that much more difficult. Not only do the authors have to peel away the myths surrounding them, they also face the harsh reality that royal staff who do talk face dismissal and possible prosecution for their pains, while friends within the charmed royal circle run the risk of banishment to the social gulag if they speak too freely.

Therefore I am all the more grateful to those necessarily anonymous staff and friends whose reminiscences have been vital in compiling this book. From within the walls of Kensington Palace, Buckingham Palace, and Windsor Castle, my thanks to Scottie, S.J.W., C.M., but especially L.S.M. and W.B.B.M. From the world of interior design, Mr Richard Jeffree and Mr Jim Smart have been invaluable guides. My thanks too to my Fleet Street colleagues, especially Fiona MacDonald Hull, James Whitaker and Neil Mackwood as well as royal authors Christopher Warwick and Trevor Hall for their detailed background knowledge, and expecially Ingrid Seward, editor of *Majesty*.

The encouragement of my publishers Michael and Lesley O'Mara and enthusiastic researcher Sarah Coombe has been everything. My thanks too to Jan Kelly for typing through the night, to Yvonne Dedman, Casey Horton, and Helena Beaufoy and to my wife Lynne for her tolerance and constructive criticism, and my daughters Alexandra and Lydia for providing the necessary dawn chorus.

Oh yes, Puccini and U2 for the background music.

Andrew Morton, *March 1987*

1

Portrait of a Palace

The rhythmic plod of measured footsteps shatters the cloistered silence of a royal courtyard. A Royal Protection Squad officer is on his evening round, walking steadily past the front doors of one of the most famous families in the world. While the last of the rush hour traffic provides a ceaseless background hum, all is quiet within the red brick walls of Kensington Palace. For once all four royal households that make their home here – the Prince and Princess of Wales, Princess Margaret, the Duke and Duchess of Gloucester, and Prince and Princess Michael of Kent – have an evening free of public engagements.

The policeman pauses for a moment under Prince Charles's first floor study as the strains of Wagner's romantic opera, *Tannhäuser*, drift across the courtyard. It is Charles's favourite work.

A light is on too in Princess Diana's sitting room. Inside, the Princess, needle in hand, is carefully embroidering a cushion as she idly follows the intrigues within the Carrington family in the television soap opera *Dynasty*. On the fifth floor Prince William and Prince Harry are sound asleep, their nanny, Ruth Wallace, on duty in the room next door.

The policeman continues his patrol along the north wing of the seventeenth-century palace, past the front door of Apartments 8 and 9, the home of the Prince and Princess of Wales, to the less substantial dwelling of their next-door neighbours, Prince and Princess Michael of Kent. From the list of names at Police Lodge he knows that tonight this royal couple are hosting a dinner party for literary friends. The sound of Princess Michael's dinner party voice – English with German inflections – cuts through the quiet. 'Michael, don't be so stupid,' she scolds. 'How could you say that?'

'She's on form tonight,' thinks the officer as he retraces his footsteps and patrols along the west wing of the palace. He walks past empty apartments once occupied by Princess Alice, Countess of Athlone. Instinctively he looks up to the Oval Window of the Clock Tower. Legend has it that on stormy nights the ghost of George II stands there, waving his fist at cruel fate. He is not on duty tonight.

Next door in Apartment 4, the home of the Duke and Duchess of Gloucester and the Duke's mother, Princess Alice, all is domestic bliss. Inside, the Danish-born Duchess is carefully dusting and rearranging her notable collection of wooden ducks. The Duke is closeted in his study, his owlish, bespectacled figure hunched intently over a glowing television screen. It is not *Dynasty* that fascinates him but the advancing army of Star Wars' monsters which he expertly shoots down using his video game console. What Shakespeare's battle-scarred Gloucester would have made of this television warrior is anyone's guess. As the protection officer passes the Gloucesters' apartment he spots the stocky figure of Princess Margaret's Polish-born cook, Stanislaw Wasneiski, hurrying down the long drive towards Kensington High Street to buy some last minute supplies. The officer smiles to himself. 'She's done it again. Swanned off to the ballet, said there would be six for supper and now there's ten.'

The policeman completes his patrol, past the portico door of Number 1A, the home of Princess Margaret, and back to Police Lodge for a cup of tea. He doesn't notice the Peter Pan figure watching him from the palace's grey slate roof. It is Princess Margaret's son, Viscount Linley, testing out security for a dare.

This then is a snapshot view of a typical evening for the royal residents of the world's most exclusive residence, Kensington Palace. The inhabitants call it variously KP, or Kens Pal. It was dubbed 'the aunt heap' by Edward VIII because so many aged relatives lived there, 'the royal ghetto' by disrespectful Americans, and 'Coronet Street' by soap opera obsessed Fleet Street. However, this royal condominium resembles not so much a modern day Versailles as an Englishman's country home thrust into great affairs. Its weathered red brick gives it a warmth and homeliness missing from the stone fronted edifice of Buckingham Palace. Yet its unassuming air is beguiling.

Kensington Palace, built by Sir Christopher Wren, has been the seat of five monarchs, the birthplace of Queen Victoria and Queen Mary, and the one-time home of the Duke of Edinburgh. While the residence has at times suffered neglect and damage it is now as important in royal life as at any time since the reign of George II more than two hundred years ago. Besides being the home of some of the most important royal households, it has gradually assumed the role of cultural, social and intellectual centre for the royal court. In the last twenty years there are few national and international figures who have not been waved through the palace security gates and up the drive. Not since the days of Addison and Pope have so many influential figures strutted across this royal stage. The wit of Noel Coward, the voice of Luciano Pavarotti, the thoughts of philosopher Sir Laurens van der Post have all been heard here.

Since Princess Margaret and Anthony Armstrong-Jones moved in at the start of the Swinging Sixties, the palace has enjoyed a renaissance as artists, musicians and politicians have wined and dined here, waxing lyrical and theoretical. Covent Garden and Westminster all pay homage at the Court of Kensington: Dame Margot Fonteyn, Rudolph Nureyev, James Callaghan and Dr David Owen are all familiar figures. When Elizabeth Taylor opened her first night in the West End show, *The Little Foxes*, she savoured her success over dinner at Princess Margaret's home. The Princess ordered her staff to applaud Miss Taylor into her apartment so that 'she would feel someone special'.

America's First Lady Nancy Reagan, entertainer Danny Kaye and television personality David Frost have all enjoyed royal hospitality. The crowned and exiled royal heads of Europe and the Middle East are regular visitors as are a stream of scientists, doctors, sociologists and philosophers. The renewed royal vigour of Kensington Palace even eclipses the glittering social life at Marlborough House in the 1890s when

the Prince of Wales, later Edward VII, entertained his phil-
istine aristocratic friends. While Princess Michael of Kent
cultivates the international jet set and the world of showbusiness, Princess Margaret patronizes the arts, particularly ballet,
opera and music.

Intellectuals and the politically influential enjoy the hospitality and patronage of Prince Charles. The Prince – perhaps
inevitably, given his constitutional position – sees himself as a
philosophical Mr Fixit, a kind of referee in the game of ideas.
The fields of alternative medicine, race relations, architecture,
the Third World, and the disabled are his special concerns.
The Prince says: 'I hope slowly but surely through various
meetings and dinners and lunches I've given that people will
get together and find that they have a certain amount in
common. They needn't necessarily view each other as bogey-
men.'

While enjoying an animated resurgence of its social life,
Kensington Palace is now unique in that, for one of the few
times in British history, so many grand and powerful royal
households are brought together to live cheek by jowl. Add to
that the Duke and Duchess of York who may take possession
of the apartment once occupied by Princess Alice, Countess of
Athlone – 'It is ideal for them,' says her biographer Theo
Aronson – and there is very nearly a royal 'full house'.

Life behind closed doors at Kensington Palace is fascinating,
for while the public see how the royal family deal with com-
moners, they never see how they get on with each other. Like
any other group, they are driven by competing vanities,
jealous of their privileges, prickly about their place in the royal
pecking order, and covetous of their possessions.

With most members of this family there is never any question of dropping in unexpectedly on one another or popping
round to borrow a cup of sugar. Communication is via private
secretaries, complaints by courteous memos. Face to face
confrontations are rare, but do occur. Their days are governed
by rigid timetables. A typical notice circulated to all of the
royal residents proclaims that 'At 11.55 am the Duchess of
Gloucester will depart from Kensington Palace for a hair
appointment at 12.15 pm.'

Their lives are set in the aspic of precedence. When they all turn out for a State banquet they leave in a set order: first the Prince and Princess of Wales, then Princess Margaret, followed by the Gloucesters and finally the Michaels. Princess Michael's lowly rank never ceases to irritate her. Yet beneath the protocol, the differences in royal personality do come quickly to the surface. The Wales don't mix with the Michaels; Princess Margaret does not speak to Princess Michael but she thinks the Gloucesters are 'sweet'. Princess Margaret will dine with Charles and Diana but make cutting remarks about the Princess to the Queen; the Duchess of Gloucester discourages her servants from mixing with the Michaels'. New staff soon get the message and quickly learn to keep quiet about friendships within the other royal 'camps'. 'We take our cues from our principals,' explained one.

Like all neighbours, the royal inhabitants are keen to learn what is happening next door and often gently pump their staff for the latest gossip. While Princess Diana has been known to hang out of the window to see who is visiting Princess Michael, none are quite so obvious as the late Princess Alice, Countess of Athlone, who insisted that her maid comb her long, grey hair in the window so that she could keep an eye on Princess Margaret. 'Ah the dear girl,' she would say. 'Wearing that same dress again. So unbecoming.'

While the Queen is not quite in the position of Louis XIV who presided over the noblemen at Versailles, she is very much in command of life at Kensington Palace. It is the Queen who decides who may borrow valuable paintings from her collection, who may use which gardens and whether a royal household may stable their horses nearby. She is an undemanding but watchful landlady. The apartments are all grace and favour residences and as such are in her gift. The fortunate few pay no rent but their respect. Lighting, heating and other domestic bills are paid by the inhabitants, the upkeep of this Grade I Listed building by the Department of the Environment. Currently it costs the taxpayers about £374,000 a year – about a tenth of the cost of running the Royal Yacht *Britannia*.

Tales of intrigue, gossip, fighting, and feuding are quickly relayed to the Queen. She often knows what is going on

within the red brick walls faster than the residents. Her network of spies is as comprehensive as any set up by Good
Queen Bess. A handful of old retainers keep their social anten-
nae twitching in her service, relaying messages to her dresser
and lifelong companion Bobo MacDonald at Buckingham
Palace. Bobo – the only servant allowed to call the Queen
'Lilibet' – soon tells her mistress the latest tittle-tattle. It is no
idle legend. When a footman, John Davis, was taken seriously
ill he was helped to the ambulance by Prince Charles's valet.
On his return the valet apologized to the Prince for being
away. 'It's alright,' said Prince Charles. 'The Queen has told
me all about it.' Barely 15 minutes had elapsed since the valet
was at the side of the stricken servant. On another occasion
Princess Alexandra commiserated with a servant for the way
he was being treated by his royal mistress. When he feigned
surprise at her knowledge, the Princess said conspiratorily
'The Queen told me.'

Just as the House of Windsor is a matriarchal family, dominated both by royal ladies and their nannies, so historically
Kensington Palace has been held under the thrall of spirited,
single-minded and ruthless women. Queen Anne, Queen
Caroline, Queen Victoria, and Queen Mary have all left their
mark on its history. Today their spirit – and occasionally their
ghosts – still haunts the palace and their iron is certainly in the
souls of the current leading ladies.

It was the behaviour of Princess Diana that inspired the
famous headline 'Malice at the Palace'. She is in control of
running Apartments 8 and 9, is mistress of the daily routine,
the staff arrangements, the menus, and the decorations. It was
her influence, and that of her mother, Mrs Frances Shand
Kydd, that was responsible for turning an apartment that
Prince Charles first dismissed as a 'pigeon loft' into an elegant
and spacious home. Intellectually questing, Prince Charles
allows his wife complete domestic control, just as in the good
old days under Nanny Anderson. Offered the choice of two
pairs of shoes in the morning, the Prince snapped at his valet 'I
pay you to choose for me.' Now it is Diana who decides.

The same donnish disregard for the material world suffuses
the domestic world of Prince Richard, the Duke of Gloucester,

and his bearded cousin Prince Michael of Kent. They too are dominated by determined wives with definite ideas on running a royal household.

Perhaps it is the influence of so many women that gives Kensington Palace its genteel, fireside quality. It is an image captured by Leigh Hunt, who wrote 'Windsor Castle is a place to receive monarchs in, Buckingham Palace to see fashion, Kensington Palace seems a place to drink tea in.'

A romantic place of secret walled gardens, sunken ponds and cobbled courtyards where the early morning mists linger – Kensington Palace has the inescapable feel of an Edwardian English country village. 'When you leave the hustle and bustle of Kensington High Street and go back into the palace it is like entering a time warp. It is so peaceful and quiet,' says one long-serving servant.

Like any village it has its own rhythm. Every day John the milkman arrives promptly at 9.30, the laundry van arrives each Wednesday, the mobile greengrocer and florist each Friday. 'I've just spent £15 on flowers,' moans Princess Michael of Kent good naturedly. 'But they make such a difference to a room, don't you think.' The warren of apartments is so complex that the Post Office always uses the same postman. Like other regular tradesmen, he is invited to the Christmas staff party. But these days Kensington Palace is not quite the friendly idyll it once was. The shadow of terrorism looms large. While residents chat and pass the time of day they are guarded by armed police, laser beams, and heat-sensitive security devices. Even royal nannies have to carry walkie talkies when they take their charges for a promenade in the same park where the young Princess Victoria would gaily pass the time of day with complete strangers.

However like any village, where feuds go hand in hand with friendship, rivalry will quickly turn to revelry on any important family occasion. When Princess Diana arrived home from St Mary's Hospital, Paddington, carrying baby Prince William, the royal staff were out in force. Mistress of ceremonies was Princess Margaret who ensured they all had something to wave. Inappropriately she chose a pink – rather than a blue – towel.

Kensington Palace is both homely yet increasingly influential, a place where court formality curls gently at the edges. But not completely – it is still a home where the children expect their parents to arrive home from work by helicopter, where a man in uniform takes them to school, and where most visitors call their parents 'Your Royal Highness'.

If George V had had his way he would have demolished the charmless royal office block of Buckingham Palace and returned Kensington Palace to its former glory as the centre of court life. Without such drastic measures Kensington Palace has achieved that status. This unassuming royal palace started life as a royal health centre. In 1689 William III bought the property and site of Nottingham House from the Earl of Nottingham for the princely sum of 18,000 guineas. The King, who suffered badly from asthma, found his palace in Whitehall unhealthy because of the notorious fogs and flooding from the Thames. However Nottingham House was too small for the paraphernalia of a royal court. Sir Christopher Wren was commissioned to enlarge and develop the site. Work began quickly but was dogged by disasters and delays. A contemporary reporter wrote: 'The additional buildings to the King's house at Kensington being newly covered with lead, fell down all of a sudden and hurt several people and killed some, the Queen herself being there but a little time before.'

A new road was built – still partly to be seen in Rotten Row (Route de Roi) – which was provided with lamp posts on either side to discourage footpads. These precautions were not sufficient for a later inhabitant, George II, who is probably the only monarch ever to have been mugged. A highwayman climbed over the wall of the palace and 'with a manner of much deference, deprived the king of his purse, his watch and his buckles'.

The first royal occupants of the palace, William and Mary, had barely settled in before a fire broke out one night. William was lucky to escape in his nightshirt, and directed the removal of pictures and other valuables, while the Queen's ladies ran around the garden screaming. In 1694 Mary was a victim of the smallpox epidemic, and rather than send for the doctors, who would have diagnosed the inevitable, she quietly settled her affairs, locked herself in her bedchamber and waited patiently for the end. The records of the palace carpenter John Churchill record a charge for 'mending ye steps of ye grt Stairs yet was broke in carrying ye Queen's body down'. William died at Kensington. He caught a chill after be broke a collar-bone as his horse stumbled on a mole hill during a ride in Hampton Court.

Queen Anne, William's successor, did not neglect Kensington Palace; the charming Orangery built in 1704-5 is her memorial. Soon after she and her obese and asthmatic consort, Prince George of Denmark, moved in, he died suddenly. The grieving Queen ordered that 'there be a great many yeoman of the guard to carry the prince's dear body, that it may not be let fall, the great stairs being very steep and slippery.'

As the centre of power, Kensington Palace was also the spring for intrigue and conspiracy. It was here that Queen Anne made her final breach with her former friend and political confidante, the domineering Sarah, Duchess of Marlborough. Harsh and bitter words were uttered in the Queen's closet and Sarah left the palace in disgrace.

The Queen died at the palace in 1714, a lonely and unhappy woman. She was succeeded by the unamiable figure of George I, who cared little about the palace, the gardens or the country.

Sir Horace Walpole was left to run the nation while 'German George' surrounded himself with a veritable circus of fellow countrymen. He brought over his plump Hanoverian mistresses and left his wife imprisoned in a remote German castle on trumped-up legal charges. For entertainment there was Jory the dwarf, a court favourite whose behaviour clearly mirrored his master's. On one occasion he was sentenced to a night of bread and water and imprisonment in the guard room (now Princess Margaret's garden room) after molesting a maid and attacking two footmen. The king also had another human 'pet' – a pathetic creature called Peter the Wild Boy who was found in the woods near Hameln in Hanover. He was allowed to roam around the palace grounds living off moss and grass, 'displaying the agility of a squirrel'.

For all his grotesque behaviour it was George I who commissioned the improvements and enlargement of the west
section of Kensington Palace, now home to the present royal
inhabitants. The reasons however were more carnal than crea-
tive. He wished to house his mistress, the Duchess of Kendal,
in some style. A handsome apartment was built along the
north west range where every night the King would visit her.
Later the King's son and successor, George II, housed two of
his own mistresses here. This former house of sin is now the
home of the Prince and Princess of Wales.

George II proved a more popular king than his father but he
left his wife, Queen Caroline, to rule at Kensington Palace.
The Queen, as Voltaire said, was 'born to encourage' and
under her patronage the arts flourished. Hogarth and Kneller
both benefited from her love of painting. Architects and
landscape gardeners won her commissions. She was responsible for overseeing work on the Serpentine and landscaping
Kensington Gardens in a form that is essentially unchanged
today. Her cultural interests made her quickly realize the
significance of a cache of drawings found in the hidden recess
of a cabinet in the palace. They were long lost sketches by
Holbein and Leonardo da Vinci which now form an important
and priceless part of the royal collection.

While artistic life flourished within the palace, so too did
petty squabbles, backbiting and bickering. The history of
Kensington Palace is littered with stories of family feuds and
infighting. It is no surprise that the present residents too have
their spats. Indeed it would be more astonishing if they all
lived in perfect harmony.

Court favourite, Lord Hervey, lovingly chronicled the
family rows that occurred during George II's reign. He noted
that once when George II joined the family circle in the gallery
he 'snubbed the Queen, who was drinking chocolate, for
being always stuffing, the Princess Emily for not hearing him,
the Princess Caroline for being grown fat, the Duke of Cumberland for standing awkwardly.'

The rooms of the palace echoed to whispered confidences,
tawdry tittle-tattle and malicious gossip. No one enjoyed it
more than Queen Caroline, who once commanded Hervey to

relay the latest news while she was in bed. As it was against Court etiquette for a gentleman to invade a lady's bedchamber, the courtier was obliged to bellow his confidences from the other side of the bedroom door. Much talk centred around the wayward behaviour of her hated son, the Prince of Wales. Even as she lay on her death bed in the palace, Queen Caroline had nothing but harsh words for her wild and wilful son. She said bitterly 'At least I shall have one comfort in having my eyes eternally closed – I shall never see that monster again.'

Even though George II had his mistresses, he missed his wife more than he first admitted. In his grief he closed half the palace and he too died there in 1760, expiring in a small room next to the water closet. His grandson and successor, George III, had no personal use for Kensington Palace and it is from this time that its long association with lesser members of the royal family dates. Unlike the residents of the royal houses at Kew and Buckingham House, Kensington Palace residents did not lead a formal court life in so far as people would not call before breakfast. By contrast the monarch was almost never alone. Some citizens had the right to his bedchamber, others the right to sit with him in the privy. This degree of access does rather overshadow the present royal family's complaints about press harassment.

At the beginning of the nineteenth century Kensington Palace stirred from its slumber. It acquired a number of distinguished and infamous royal residents and once more became the centre of social and political life. One of the palace's great eccentrics was George III's sixth son, Augustus Frederick, later the Duke of Sussex. The Duke, who was as vain as he was odd, always wore a skull cap to prevent catching a chill and wandered the palace in one of his extensive collection of silk dressing gowns. He had a voice which, he boasted, could span three octaves and he would sing to the finches which he allowed to fly free around his apartments. However he made a significant contribution to national life. He had a much admired collection of 5000 rare Bibles and manuscripts which he housed in a specially built Divinity Room. True to character he left his body to science, declaring that he did not believe a word of the Christian faith. He was a consistent supporter of his notorious neighbour, Caroline, the Princess of Wales. Her marriage to the Prince of Wales, later George IV, was a disaster and the talk of London society; he deserted her soon after their daughter, Princess Charlotte, was born. Their hatred was mutual and reflected in the country as a whole. The mob supported either Caroline and Sussex or Darling Prinnie – the nickname for the Prince of Wales.

In 1808 George III granted Caroline apartments at Kensington Palace where distinguished guests such as Sir Walter Scott, Lord Byron, Lord Eldon, and Spencer Percival, paid court to her. They just as soon spurned her when her unconventional habits of 'walking hatless and talking on a bench to strangers' shocked polite society. She even suffered the humiliation of being refused entry to her husband's coronation. The death of her much loved daughter, Princess Charlotte, broke her heart, and the outcast Princess passed away several years later. She was a tragic, unhappy figure, and it is therefore no surprise that she is one of a triumvirate of ghosts which are said to haunt Kensington Palace.

The oldest spirit is that of George II, whose moaning ghost nearly led to a mutiny among the Kensington Palace guards. During the nineteenth century one sentry on duty in the inner court was startled out of his wits to see the figure of the long dead king approaching, and was moved 'to thrust at it with his bayonet'. After this incident the men refused to stand guard in this part of the palace.

The spirit of George II is most often sighted in the Oval Window of the Clock Tower. According to legend the ghost goes abroad on windy, autumnal nights when its anxious face is seen to press itself against the panes and the lips move as if it were talking to itself. All the time the figure stares at the weather vane on the Cupola. The reason for his obsession with the weather is that in his last years all this lonely and widowed king had to look forward to were letters from home. If the wind blew the wrong way the packet boat would not sail and the longed-for letters would be delayed.

Another ghost was a contemporary of Caroline, Princess of Wales. It is that of Princess Sophia, George III's delicate and near-blind daughter who moved into Kensington Palace in 1820. From time to time the sound of a spinning wheel, her only pleasure in life, is said to come from her former apartments. But it is the plaintive and forlorn spirit of Princess Caroline for which there is more contemporary evidence. Her ghost haunts the apartments now occupied by Princess Margaret. However the Princess is severely sceptical of such suggestions. When asked about it she said: 'There is only one Princess who lives in this house and that is me. My house is not haunted.'

Her staff are not convinced. On one occasion Margaret's housekeeper, the late Jean McIntyre, was waiting in the stone-flagged entrance hall for the Princess to arrive back from an engagement. Mrs Mack, as she was known, was making sure everything was in order when she chanced to look up to the drawing room door which leads off the entrance hallway. In the doorway was the shrouded figure of a woman in a striped satin Regency dress, of the type favoured by Princess Caroline. The face was unclear and in an instant it was gone. Princess Margaret's guest bedroom is also a favourite for this royal ghost. One day Scottish-born Mrs Mack was dusting the figurines which adorn the dressing table. After she finished her work she carefully replaced each one on the polished top. As she was leaving the bedroom something made her turn. To her horror she watched as a china figure swayed backwards and forwards before falling over. A draught of wind – or evidence of a spiritual presence?

On another occasion two carpenters were working near the same guest room. While one was engrossed in his work he felt the presence of someone, who he presumed to be his colleague, standing near him. He asked him to pass a tool. There was no response. He repeated his request, this time in a louder voice. Again there was no answer. At the moment he turned his colleague called 'I don't know what you are shouting at me for, I'm working downstairs.'

The most chilling experience occurred late one night. Mrs Mack and another member of staff lived in separate apartments at the top floor of the house. They had retired to their respective bedrooms and were just settling down for the night when the silence was split by a blood-curdling scream. Both quickly dragged on their dressing gowns, and calling 'Don't worry, I'm coming', raced down the shared corridor. They met in the middle to discover that neither had uttered a sound. There was no one else in the house that night.

While the ghost of Princess Caroline may still make her presence felt, Kensington Palace is better remembered as the birthplace of her niece, Queen Victoria. It was her birth at the palace on Monday 24 May 1819, which, during her early life, underpinned the palace's position as a rival to the courts of George IV and William IV. The palace once more became a place of intrigue and collusion as its political importance grew. With the death of Princess Charlotte and the inability of George III's children to provide an heir, the race was on to maintain the royal line.

The heir of Edward, Duke of Kent, George III's fourth son, was an obvious contender for the throne. After the Duke's marriage to the plump and widowed Princess Victoire of Coburg, Dowager Princess of Leiningen, the couple lived for a time at her home in Germany. When she became pregnant, the Duke, realizing the possible dynastic consequences, was determined that his wife should give birth to their child in England.

Heavily in debt, the Duke borrowed £15,000 from friends to travel to England and to make ready his apartments at Kensington Palace. Although the birth was not expected for six weeks, by the travelling standards of the day this was not overgenerous. Their journey was slowed down by a baggage train which included an enormous bed (should the Duchess's labour start in the middle of the Channel), and the fact that the Duke insisted on driving the coach himself to save money. The party fretted for a week at Calais because of unfavourable winds, but on 29 April 1819 they embarked, hastened by brisk winds which saw them across the Channel in three hours and made the wretched Duchess abominably seasick.

They reached London to find the apartment in a state of disarray, and the unfortunate Duchess had to give birth in the Duke's dressing room. The birth of the future Queen brought to the surface tensions between the Prince Regent – later George IV – and the Kents. This boil of family malevolence burst at the infant's christening, held in the Cupola Room at Kensington Palace a month after the birth.

In accordance with Court protocol, a letter had already been submitted to the Regent with the proposed names for the child – Georgina Charlotte Augusta Alexandrina Victoria. The night before the christening the Prince Regent sent a message to the Duke disallowing the name Georgina. On the day of the christening the Archbishop of Canterbury held the baby Princess in his arms, waiting patiently for the Regent to give her a name. The Regent remained silent for an eternity. Finally he said gruffly 'Alexandrina.' The Duke then suggested: 'Charlotte?' The Regent shook his head at the mention of his dead daughter's name. 'Augusta?' asked the Duke, his mood turning to anger. This too was refused. 'Elizabeth?' Again no. The Duchess began to cry and the Archbishop looked from Duke to Prince, wondering if this sorry charade would ever end. There was another long silence, broken only by the Duchess's sobbing. Finally the Regent shouted: 'Call her after her mother.' And that was that. The woman who would become the grandmother of modern Europe began life as Alexandrina Victoria, known for the first nine years of her life as 'Drina'.

The grotesque christening scene was but a harbinger of the rivalries to come, as relations between the inhabitants of Kensington Palace and the official court grew ever more bitter. The young Princess however was shielded from these rivalries both by her youth and her mother. Indeed, following her father's death nine months after her birth, Victoria slept in the same room as her mother.

In reminiscences written in 1872 Queen Victoria described her childhood as 'rather melancholy' but the early days seem happy enough. Her first recollections were of crawling on a yellow carpet at Kensington Palace and being told that if she was naughty and cried her 'Uncle Sussex' who lived in the next apartment would hear her and punish her. She recalled: 'For which reason I always screamed when I saw him.' She was also terrified of bishops with their flowing robes, wigs and aprons, but overcame her fear when the Bishop of Salisbury, Dr Fisher, got down on the floor and let her play with his badge of Chancellor of the Order of the Garter. She had a simple daily routine – breakfast at half-past eight, lunch at half-past one and dinner at seven – and few friends who were her own age.

Victoria, dubbed 'Little Mayflower' became a focus of public interest and was a familiar figure parading around Kensington Gardens on the back of a donkey given to her by the Duke of York. On one occasion there was near disaster during a ride in her pony carriage. The carriage was upset when a dog gambolled between the legs of the pony. As the Princess was falling out a soldier grabbed her and pulled her to safety. He was given a guinea as a reward.

When the Princess was seven, Lord Albemarle observed her, wearing a straw hat and cotton dress, watering the plants in the palace garden. He wrote: 'It was amusing to see how impartially she divided the contents of the watering pot between the flowers and her own little feet.' Sweet though she may have seemed to onlookers, the Princess was spoilt by her doting mother. Her table manners left much to be desired; she shouted 'I want' at servants as she crammed hot buttered toast into her mouth, picked at bones and regularly slurped three bowls of soup at a sitting.

While the growing child showed an aptitude for languages, art and painting, it was during a history lesson at the palace that she first learned of her future role. An extra page had been deliberately inserted into a book on the kings and queens of England, with her name following those of George IV and William IV. She wept a little at the discovery and told her governess Baroness Lehzen: 'I will be good.'

William IV was fond of his niece and heir, but he loathed the possessive Duchess and the man who held her under his spell, her private secretary Sir John Conroy. It was his intrigues which led to the deepening rift between the Court and Kensington Palace. The quarrel with the King came to a head in August 1836 when William IV secretly visited Kensington Palace while the residents were away. He was furious to discover that the Duchess and her entourage had annexed an extra seventeen rooms. At his birthday dinner at Windsor Castle he publicly rebuked the Duchess for keeping his heir away from Court, saying 'The person now near me is surrounded by evil advisors.'

In the atmosphere of intrigue surrounding Victoria any farfetched rumour was believed by the Duchess. She was alarmed when Conroy convinced her that the Duke of Cumberland planned to poison her daughter's milk so that he could inherit the throne. The Duchess was so concerned by wild stories in the press saying that Victoria was too ill to walk that she forced the Princess to take public promenades in Kensington Gardens. Throughout these endless machinations, Victoria kept aloof from Conroy. This provoked him to fury. He tried to force her to accept him as her private secretary when she became Queen, even asking the Duchess to lock her in her room until she gave way. He failed in his ambition – but not without a fight. On 20 June 1837 King William IV died at Windsor, and the Archbishop of Canterbury and the Lord Chamberlain, Lord Conyngham, set out for Kensington. There were nerve wracking delays as first they found the lodge gates shut and the porter snoring, and then their way barred by the obdurate Duchess, adamant that no one could be allowed into her daughter's presence as she was asleep. Finally the Duchess consented to awake the 'dear child with a kiss' and led her through the anteroom to the King's Backstairs. For the last time they descended the slippery steps together, the Duchess carrying a silver candlestick, and Victoria's tutor, a bottle of smelling salts. In her dressing gown, Victoria was led to the sitting room where Lord Conyngham announced the news, then knelt and kissed the hand of his new Queen. It was the end of an era and the start of a new dynasty.

While Britain thrived under Victoria, her birthplace was in a state of royal eclipse. Although fond of her home, the Queen soon moved to Buckingham Palace – the first monarch to occupy it. Here she enjoyed the unaccustomed luxury of her own bedroom. Conroy was dismissed; her mother lived on but her influence waned to that of mere irritation.

On 13 July 1837 the Queen recorded her departure from Kensington Palace in her diary. 'Though I rejoice to go into Buckingham Palace for many reasons it is not without feelings of regret that I shall bid adieu forever to my birthplace. . . . I have seen my sister married here [Princess Feodore of Hohenlohe, her half sister who married when Victoria was nine], I have seen many of my dear relations here, I have had pleasant balls and delicious concerts here. I have gone through painful and disagreeable scenes here 'tis true, but I am fond of the poor old Palace.' Her affection is illustrated by the fact that she conferred pensions on a number of old retainers, including the crossing sweeper outside Kensington Palace.

While Queen Victoria rarely visited Kensington Palace it was often in her mind, and it was due to her chiding and chivvying of government departments that it remained intact. She firmly resisted suggestions that it should be made the site of the National Gallery and instead kept those rooms which were inhabitable filled with royal relations.

In 1867 another May baby with a regal destiny was born at Kensington Palace in the very room, the King's State Bedchamber, where Queen Victoria had been woken by her mother on the morning of the Accession. She was Princess Victoria Mary of Teck, known as Princess May, whose mother, a plump chatterbox of a woman, was the Queen's cousin, Princess Mary Adelaide of Cambridge. The Tecks were incorrigible spendthrifts and soon ran up a mountain of debts with local traders. Fat Mary, as she was called, was so blithely indifferent to her balance sheet that when she opened a new church hall in Kensington she singled out a local grocer for praise in her speech. 'And now I propose a special vote of thanks to Mr Barker to whom we all owe so much.'

The feckless family were so overdrawn that they were forced to leave the country for a time. However Queen Mary never forgot her mother's lavish hospitality and remembered as a child how she loved to peep at the guests arriving for glittering dinner parties in the Red Saloon.

Gradually the palace took on the character of fading gentility as Victoria granted rooms to her daughters or to retired retainers. Much of the correspondence of the period was not so much about great matters of state as the state of the wallpaper and the condition of the drains. It is a subject that still vexes today's royal inhabitants.

In 1873 the Queen's talented but shy sixth daughter, Princess Louise, was given rooms formerly occupied by the Duchess of Inverness, widow of the Duke of Sussex. Until her death in 1939 the Princess, a sculptress, occupied the apartments now used by Princess Margaret. When Princess Margaret moved in she found a dark, rather forbidding house, redolent of aspidistras, brown varnish and oppressive Victorian stuffiness.

Princess Louise, who had a studio at the palace, did make one dramatic change to her apartments. In the garden room at this time there were three large windows. When she discovered that her husband, Lord Lorne, was climbing through one of the windows at night to meet his mistress she ordered it to be bricked up.

Domestic upheavals aside, Princess Louise's greatest contribution to Kensington Palace was her fine statue of Queen Victoria in her coronation robes, which now stands in the Broad Walk.

Thankfully, palace routine was refreshingly free from the suffocating constraints of Victorian court life. Princess Louise and her husband lived simply, dining off baked potatoes, meat and vegetables, although the Princess always drew a sketch for the cook to show him how the finished meal should look.

In their small chintzy drawing room the couple entertained their friends and relations. The relaxed atmosphere was in stark contrast to the prevailing mood at Osborne and Balmoral, where Queen Victoria would sit in the centre of the room in one large chair while the rest of the family sat round in smaller chairs. Topics of conversation were pre-arranged and no one spoke unless bidden. Coughing or sneezing were considered to be socially disgraceful as the talk followed its tortuous course.

During Louise's tenancy much of the palace was allowed to decay. Some of the State rooms were used as barracks; the King's Gallery was relegated to a coal store and boot room. Fortunately parliament came to its senses and voted £23,000 for restoration work. The work was undertaken on the basis that the State Apartments would be open to the public. Appropriately the day scheduled for the official opening co-incided with Queen Victoria's 80th birthday, 24 May 1899. Several days before this she paid her final visit to the restored apartments. The now frail Queen failed to recognize many of her old haunts as she was carried through the palace in a bathchair.

With Queen Victoria's death, Kensington Palace lost a benign benefactor. However Queen Mary was hovering in the wings as its new guardian angel. Testimony to her interest was the grand plan for the palace dreamed up by her husband, George V. In 1912 Lord Esher wrote 'King George's dream . . . is to pull down Buckingham Palace, to round off St James and the Green Park at Constitution Hill and Buckingham Gate and with the money obtained by the sale of the gardens of Buckingham Palace to reconstruct Kensington Palace as the town residence of the Sovereign.' It remained a delicious dream. Landscaping work continued and in 1911, as more of the State Apartments were opened to the public, Kensington Palace housed the London Museum. However, the western section of the palace remained the preserve of the royal res-idents. Princess Beatrice, Queen Victoria's youngest daughter and devoted companion, acquired an apartment next door to her sister, Princess Louise, while in 1917 her sister-in-law, the Duchess of Albany, moved into the Clock House. Her daughter Princess Alice, Countess of Athlone, lived there until 1981.

During World War I the palace resembled a military camp after George V allowed a number of rooms to be used by those working for Irish prisoners of war and Irish soldiers at the front. Thousands of food parcels were sent off each week and the King insisted that the palace share the same rations as everyone else. Princess Louise told one friend that she stuck to the rules: 'Georgie would never forgive me if I didn't.'

As a sign of the changing times the Princess found that she could no longer afford to travel about London in taxis. Instead she caught the red double-decker London Transport buses which still pass by the palace gates. Worried about possible offences against royal protocol she asked George V if it was appropriate. He replied in shocked tones 'What would Grandmama have thought? Do you strap hang?' He assigned her an ancient Daimler to spare her the indignity of mixing with the common herd.

In the 1920s and 30s Kensington Palace was truly an 'aunt heap'. One ritual epitomizes the atmosphere of a royal rest home. Every Wednesday night Princess Louise went to Durrant's, a West End hotel, so that she could sit on a bed with two old friends, Mrs Savory and Mrs Anthony Gibbs. As they chatted about the old days of Victoria and the Kaiser they sipped neat gin out of an old tooth mug.

The arrival of a boisterous little boy, living in exile from Greece, brought some much needed 'vim' to the palace. He was the young Prince Philip, and over the years he lived on and off with his aged relatives – 'Kensington Palace was a sort of base where I kept my things', he says. He stayed with his grandmother, the Dowager Marchioness of Milford Haven, a stern Victorian never without a book or cigarette in her hand. His grandmother's neighbour, Princess Alice, Countess of Athlone, observed 'She looked like a rag bag, just scraping her hair back anyhow. She had a natural talent for passing on knowledge and drawing people in conversation. But her heavy smoking gave her a harsh coarse voice.'

It was here that the young Prince learned to walk, and, like generations of royal children, was a regular visitor to Kensington Gardens. On one occasion the Prince was taken to the cinema by Mountbatten's footman, Charles Smith. They were given six shillings for tea and cinema tickets. As an extra treat Philip was allowed to ride on the top of the double-decker bus. They went to see *Treasure Island* at the Victoria Metropole but while Smith's back was turned, Philip picked up a wad of sticky 'reserved' labels. The next day they appeared on every lavatory door in the royal apartments.

As a lively eight-year-old Philip went out into Kensington High Street and bought himself a trumpet, only to be told not to blow it inside because the discordant noise would wake his ageing aunts.

Philip and his friend, the young Marquis of Milford Haven, often climbed in over the palace roofs and through a skylight so they would not disturb the sleeping grandmother. If they came in through the front door they knew from bitter experience that the creaking floorboards would make too much noise for them to escape discovery. One night a patrolling policeman saw the royal cat burglar on the roof and ordered him to climb down. Philip refused – and defied the officer to come and catch him.

During the war he stayed at Kensington Palace on leave from the Navy, but it was a sad and lost place. The pictures had been taken into storage, the furniture covered in dust sheets. The palace suffered during the war; it was hit by incendiary bombs in October 1940 and later by a flying bomb. The gardens sprouted anti-aircraft guns, sandbags and trenches, while the palace became the headquarters of No 34 Personnel Section.

In 1964 Princess Alice, Countess of Athlone, saw the damage when she returned from Canada where the Earl of Athlone had been Governor General. She has written 'Our apartments were in complete chaos. The disastrous fire has destroyed part of our roof and attic rooms. No window frames were left and all our furniture, books and pictures were heaped higgledy-piggledy in the drawing rooms.... As everywhere else help was unprocurable ... Aunt May [Queen Mary] even came to help wash China.'

That afternoon's work by the Queen is well remembered by Ernest Bennett, formerly the Queen's Page, who now lives in retirement at Kensington Palace. He and Queen Mary worked in the kitchen together, washing the dust off the bone china. He washed, she wiped. 'She was very good,' he remembers. 'She didn't actually dry the china, she patted it. Of course it took all afternoon to wash a dinner service.'

The palace, careworn and battered by war, was once more thrust into the spotlight when Prince Philip married Princess Elizabeth, now the Queen, at Westminster Abbey in 1947. After the engagement was announced he went to live at Kensington Palace, sleeping in rooms as spartan as his own wardrobe. His former valet John Dean recalls that the Prince only had one suit, three uniforms and socks full of darned holes. On the morning of the wedding Philip had toast and coffee and then joined his best man, Lord Milford Haven, in a gin and tonic to calm his nerves. Before leaving he made a point of saying goodbye to the Kensington Palace chimney sweep.

The year before, a sale of the furniture, silver, pictures, and books belonging to Princess Beatrice – who died in 1944 – was held at the palace. One visitor remembers the extraordinary number of silver asparagus holders up for auction. The bombings, the departure of Philip and the deaths of Queen Victoria's daughters, Louise and Beatrice, closed a chapter in the palace's history. It was a period of neglect and decay, when the palace languished in the forgotten backwaters of royal life.

A new era began in 1955 with the arrival of Princess Marina, the widow of Prince George, Duke of Kent, who was killed in a flying accident during the war. Like a phoenix the palace rose from the ashes.

The Princess moved in with her three children, Prince Edward, Duke of Kent, Prince Michael and Princess Alexandra. That October, for the first time in years, a Court Circular was issued from Kensington Palace announcing a royal engagement.

Although living in straitened circumstances, Princess Marina brought a refreshing style and elegance to royal life. However, Princess Michael of Kent is convinced that Princess Marina's taste came from her husband. She says: 'The late Duke of Kent designed a lot of things. He was the only one of Queen Mary's children who had a love of beautiful objects. He was really the creator of Princess Marina's style. When she arrived in England she was decidedly dowdy. It was under his guidance that she became a fashion Princess.'

The occasional sale of family silver and Fabergé ornaments kept the family in reasonable comfort, although the Princess never forgot – nor would let her children forget – their royal station. When Angus Ogilvy married her daughter Princess Alexandra he introduced her to his friends simply as Alexandra. Princess Marina got to hear of this and rang him from her palace apartments. 'I have been informed that at your dinner parties you are introducing my daughter as Alexandra. This really will not do. If the mystique of the monarchy is to be maintained my daughter must be introduced as Princess Alexandra and afterwards referred to as Ma'am.' Ogilvy obliged and had the embarrassing task of telling his friends about the edict.

Within her apartments Princess Marina was a stickler for details; every piece of Meissen, every item of furniture had its correct position – a trait that Princess Michael of Kent now displays. The butler always answered the door – except when family came to call. The front door was left open for visits from the Queen, Queen Mother and Prince Philip. They often brought along young Prince Charles who would entertain the company by playing his violin before being led to the kitchen for tea.

Princess Marina fretted for days before dinner parties, worrying about menus and seating arrangements. Douglas Fairbanks, Sir Malcolm Sargent and Noel Coward were regular guests. Even Churchill came to visit. Her butler, Peter Russell, remembers the occasion when Noel Coward was singing and playing the piano and Prince Edward's dog, Columbia, went up to the instrument and piddled against the leg. Noel Coward chortled with mirth and said 'You see, not only an actor but a critic too.'

While Princess Marina entertained the rich and famous, she liked to go incognito when she travelled from Kensington Palace. She loved nothing more than to put on a headscarf and an old coat and walk in the palace gardens. On one occasion she was approached by two American tourists while she was out walking her dog. At first she thought they were going to ask if they could take a picture of her. Instead they asked if she would take a picture of them sitting on a park bench. Highly amused, the Princess later told her friends 'I wouldn't have known how to focus it if I hadn't owned one myself of the same make.' While essentially a minor member of the royal family Princess Marina rekindled interest in the palace, interest which was further fanned by the arrival of Princess Margaret and Antony Armstrong-Jones in the early 1960s. Their residence coincided with the Kennedy presidency and many saw parallels between the wind of change blowing through American society and this artistic couple who seemed to represent a vibrant, glamorous image of royalty that was acceptable to the Swinging Sixties generation.

However, the new guard were still in a minority, living alongside courtiers such as the Master of the Horse, the Duke of Beaufort, and the Queen's private secretary Sir Alan Lascelles. It was Sir Alan who engineered the end of Princess Margaret's ill-fated romance with the divorcé Group Captain Peter Townsend. Sir Alan lived on to a ripe old age in spite of the fact that his near neighbour, Princess Margaret, refused to speak to him and 'cursed him to the grave' for his treachery.

Living on too was Princess Alice, Countess of Athlone, the last of Queen Victoria's grandchildren. She became such a fixture that she was known locally as 'the grand old lady of Kensington'. She regularly caught the No 9 bus rather than use an official car and every day went to see her friend Ada Shakespeare selling flowers in Kensington High Street.

Princess Alice could be imperiously Victorian. When the Queen came to visit, the irascible old lady called out 'Turn the heater off when you go out.' On another occasion she kept Queen Juliana of the Netherlands waiting while she enjoyed a piece of chocolate cake with her friends at a local Derby and Joan club. When friends asked her to use a walking stick she reluctantly agreed but on condition that it was disguised as an umbrella. Even her death had its comic moments. The day before her funeral in January 1981 a party of Lifeguards, who were pallbearers, rehearsed carrying the lead-lined coffin from her Kensington Palace home to Frogmore at Windsor where she was to be buried. Instead of using the coffin they carried a concrete slab weighted down with sandbags. With much huffing and puffing they managed to load the weight into the funeral car. All went well until they were lowering the slab into the grave at Frogmore. Suddenly the earth sides gave way and the men went tumbling into the grave, ropes and all. On the day of the funeral the graveside was shored up with sturdy wooden planks.

Entering the apartments left by the Princess was like entering a time capsule. Nothing had been modernized or altered since before the war. The entire interior of the house was painted pale green – the Queen Mother's favourite colour – and was full of Victoriana, including a superb collection of old silk fans.

As in many other families, some members of the royal family possess a magpie instinct that surfaces when an aged relative dies and leaves a house full of fascinating furniture and artefacts. When the Dowager Marchioness of Milford Haven died at Kensington Palace in 1950, her daughter, Queen Louise of Sweden, spent hours sifting through her possessions. Her lack of sentiment for her departed mother's memory shocked her niece. She watched in horror as the Queen ripped out the flyleaves of the Duchess's books. All bore valuable inscriptions from Queen Victoria. As Queen Louise tore out the pages she scoffed 'Do you think I'd want to have a book in my personal library just because it had Queen Victoria's signature on the flyleaf? That wouldn't make it more interesting to read.'

The same rifling of once prized possessions took place when Princess Alice, Countess of Athlone, died. This time it was a race between two next-door neighbours, Princess Michael of Kent and Prince Charles. Princess Michael won. As one member of staff said: 'She came away from the house loaded down with the equivalent of a supermarket trolley full of stuff.' Among her booty was an elephant's foot – which later ended up in the police lodge – and a pile of superb heavily embroidered linen of the type much sought after today. Prince Charles, who covets good linen, had already earmarked it for his new home and was distinctly displeased at being outdone by his new neighbour. It did not auger well for their future royal relations.

2

Making of a Royal Home

The Prince and Princess of Wales

A group of men from the Ministry, identical in their pin-striped suits, waited patiently in a gravel courtyard at Kensington Palace. They were armed with portfolios of plans, sketches and photographs, fully expecting a fusillade of questions. At precisely two o'clock, right on time, three cars pulled up; out spilled Prince Charles and a flush of detectives, equerries and private secretaries. The Prince was about to make his first major tour of inspection of Apartments 8 and 9 at Kensington Palace, which were now earmarked as his future London home. The officials from the Department of the Environment were eager to parade this renovated property.

Sadly, the Prince, a reluctant recruit to the royal condominium, was distinctly unimpressed on his first visit. His mood was not helped when his new next-door neighbour, Princess Michael of Kent, unexpectedly joined the party. Immediately she buttonholed the most senior Government official and launched into a blitzkreig of complaint. 'When are you going to fix my drains?' she asked pointedly as the group marched inside. 'My guttering is falling down and you have done nothing about it. I've been writing to you for weeks.'

The Prince, ever a gentleman, let her gatecrashing pass for the moment. As various officials pointed out to the Prince the places where dry rot, fungus, damp, and bomb damage had been rectified, Princess Michael continually interrupted their discourse, as she nagged them with her own problems. 'Nothing has been done,' she kept saying. Her plight is one that every tenant has faced with a landlord. But Charles, confronted with his own busy timetable and concerned with

33

the task in hand, lost patience. Finally he suggested politely but firmly that she take up her worries at another time. The Princess finally took the hint and went – but not before she had secured the promise of an immediate visit from the senior officials. Her harangue lasted thirty-five disruptive minutes, but she got what she came for. Charles, angered by the royal interloper, was pessimistic about the property, although he praised the work of restoration. 'It is just like a pigeon loft,' he moaned after he had looked over the three-storey building. 'Changes will have to be made.' He was concerned that the ceilings were too low for comfort and many rooms too small. He particularly wanted a master bedroom that would accommodate his fourposter bed which he had at Buckingham Palace.

It was a temporary setback for the architects who had spent four years since 1975 restoring the property to its former glory. They had successfully welded Apartments 8 and 9 into one, and turned a former passageway into the imposing porticoed front door. Their task had been made more difficult by the absence of any detailed plans. 'It was just like an Agatha Christie mystery,' recalls one senior architect. 'We had to puzzle out the layout of the historical rooms from old photographs.' Indeed all they had to guide them was a yellowing 1928 copy of *Country Life* which had photographed the interior, government pictures of the apartment taken after the bomb damage during World War II, and family photographs taken by the previous occupant, the Countess Granville.

The Countess had lived at Kensington Palace through four reigns and nearly fifty years, sharing the apartments with two spinster ladies known as the Misses Kerr who fed the sparrows from their windows. In their day sheep had grazed on Kensington Green beneath what is now the front of the Prince and Princess of Wales's home.

The Countess, who was the mother-in-law of the Queen Mother's sister Rose, was away when the apartment was hit by an incendiary bomb in 1940. Damage to her home was considerable and the shelves of the splendid Georgian library were only saved thanks to the efforts of the fire brigade. However the apartment suffered considerable water damage.

The superb Georgian staircase – dating back to 1723 – remained essentially intact although much of the fine William Kent plasterwork was blown apart or destroyed afterwards when a flying bomb hit the palace later in the war.

Like a rotten core at the heart of Kensington Palace, Apartments 8 and 9 remained empty, neglected and slowly collapsing. It was not until 1975 that the Queen and her advisors decided that it was time to make a start on the derelict northwest wing of the private apartments. The apartments were in a forlorn state. Only a rough corrugated roof stopped the rain coming in and it was no surprise to find the apartments riddled with damp and rot. Sir Horace Walpole commented on the damp when he visited these same apartments – then used by George II's mistress, the Duchess of Kendal – two hundred years earlier. He observed mushrooms sprouting from the floor.

The reconstruction work took six years and cost the Government £900,000. But the final result is a marvellous example of modern British craftsmanship. The 'broad and beautiful' staircase was so well renovated that you cannot tell the original from the reproduction. Where necessary the original ornate plaster ceilings were simplified but the feel of the house remained grandly Georgian. The renovation did not delight everyone however. Next-door neighbour Princess Michael of Kent was at times annoyed by the noise, particularly in the afternoon when her first baby, Lord Frederick Windsor, was having his afternoon nap. She complained particularly when the carpenters were hammering away and often they would be instructed to change to a quieter job while the baby was sleeping. Even so she took a proprietorial interest in the work, bringing daytime visitors – Lord Mountbatten was a regular – to see the progress being made.

In those pre-Diana days the central idea behind the renovation was to move Prince Charles lock, stock and barrel from his apartments at Buckingham Palace. This would have allowed him to have his office and London home in the same building, in much the same way as the Gloucesters and the Michaels operate today. On the original plan the basement was designed to hold six offices, to house his private secretary, press officer, equerry and secretaries. This scheme was approved by the Queen who visited the apartments during the reconstruction, once after seeing the ailing Princess Alice, Countess of Athlone, in her home. However the grand design was vetoed by Princess Diana who argued strongly that the apartments were too small to accommodate extra office staff and leave room for a family. She was also set against the idea of living 'above the shop'. Charles conceded the argument. Consequently the Wales's offices are housed in the south wing of Buckingham Palace where they can use the post and printing facilities. Their courtiers spend a great deal of time commuting between the two palaces, and indeed, when they hold their biannual planning meetings, they turn the dining room at Kensington Palace into a boardroom.

During the rebuilding of Kensington Palace the Prince faced considerable domestic upheaval. Not only was he overseeing the work at Apartments 8 and 9 he was also wrestling with the problem of his country house of Chevening in Kent. He was unhappy with the mansion because of the absence of any decent local hunts, the poor roads to London and the consequent additional number of helicopter journeys he had to undertake. The Prince was on the prowl for a property in the West Country – perfect hunting country and near his sister, Princess Anne, and his friends, the Parker-Bowles. When Highgrove, the Gloucestershire home of publisher and Conservative Member of Parliament Maurice Macmillan and his wife, came on the market he went to look around, making an appointment under the name of Mr Brown. He was impressed by the 350 acre property. Charles, unused to the world of commerce, never quibbled about the price of £800,000; he only paused to ask the bearer of the royal cheque book if he could afford it. The deal was promptly signed and the Prince spent a great deal of time commuting between Highgrove and Kensington Palace – as well as finding the odd moment to romance Lady Diana Spencer.

All of this played havoc with his culinary arrangements at Buckingham Palace. He was forever tucking in to a picnic lunch or dinner 'on site', as he pored over plans and discussed architectural and decorating problems. One evening the

Prince announced to his detective, John MacLean, and a Buckingham Palace valet that they would all 'pitch in' for an evening meal and do the washing up together. The Prince was elected to make the dessert, a strange concoction called banana treacle pie which he boasted he had made successfully in his rooms at Cambridge University. He caused absolute chaos in the kitchen, and as soon as the meal was over he and the detective skulked away, leaving the unfortunate servant to clear up. So much for equality.

As part of the condition of sale of Highgrove he had also bought pieces of furniture, carpets and curtains from the previous middle-aged owner. One day he proudly showed his new home to his future bride and prospective mother-in-law, Mrs Frances Shand Kydd. She was not impressed by what she saw. 'My daughter cannot live here,' she sniffed. 'It looks just like an old woman's house.' Which was exactly what it had been.

Mrs Shand Kydd promptly recommended an interior decorator for Highgrove and Kensington Palace who had done work for herself and her second husband, wallpaper magnate Peter Shand Kydd. He was the South African-born designer Dudley Poplak. It was a choice which found favour with the Queen, who had commissioned him to work on several rooms at Buckingham Palace. Poplak, discreet and retiring but rather formidable, had that extra essential quality – he was part of the royal charmed circle. He regularly escorted Queen Helen of Rumania before she died and was well known to the Mountbatten clan, particularly fellow-designer David Hicks. Indeed Hicks, who decorated Princess Anne's Gatcombe Park home, was rather disappointed not to receive the glamorous royal commission himself.

Poplak was an inspired choice that was to have a profound effect on the royal couple, particularly Diana.

The commission was prestigious but peculiarly demanding; afterwards Poplak confided to friends that he felt that he had spent 'two years before the mast'. First there were the clients. He was faced with a twenty-year-old Princess of Wales who had, quite understandably, an immature sense of interior design yet whose upbringing – she had spent some years at the

Spencer family seat of Althorp, which is bigger than any royal country home – had brought her into contact with the grand and palatial. At the same time Prince Charles was a man with simple tastes. Yet he had pronounced views on what he did not like, and, like many of us, was rather hazy about what he did want. At Chevening part of his unhappiness stemmed from the decoration which, although elegant, was not to his taste. The royal family are not noted for their interest in interior design. They prefer living in crumbling but comfortable country houses like Balmoral where in some rooms the wallpaper dates back to Queen Victoria.

There was also the problem of money, which Prince Charles made clear was not unlimited. Normally, clients who take on an interior designer of this calibre are prepared to pay between £30,000 and £40,000 for decorating a single room. In this case the more extravagant and costly ideas had to be shelved. Prince Charles was also keen to use as much British-made material as possible, as he was acutely aware that his home would be a showcase that would be visited by VIPs from overseas. At the same time Mr Poplak had the headache of incorporating furniture, carpets and antiques that clashed stylistically but had to be used because they were wedding gifts.

The newly married couple, who received an estimated ten million pounds worth of wedding presents, decided that, broadly, they would put official gifts from states and governments into Kensington Palace, while gifts from family and friends would go to Highgrove.

Another design consideration was nearer to home – Princess Michael of Kent. The Princess, an accomplished interior decorator in her own right, had already irritated the royal couple when she visited them at Highgrove shortly after it was completed. 'Charming,' she told them. 'But why didn't you let me do the decorating?' They need not have been quite so alarmed. At dinner parties Princess Michael regularly used to try to hook prospective clients with this gambit. During one affair hosted by her friend and mentor, publisher George Weidenfeld, she gaily produced her business card when the artist Graham Sutherland innocently mentioned that he wanted to make some changes to his home in the south of France.

There was an awareness, whispered *sotto voce*, that the Wales's new home at Kensington had to stand comparison with other royal apartments, which, by strange coincidence, were all being redecorated at this time. In particular, Diana did not wish to mirror Princess Michael's style – a feeling echoed by the Duchess of Gloucester who specifically instructed her decorator not to choose anything that was the same as Princess Michael's. These wishes were explained to Mr Poplak during lengthy meetings on site. The couple discussed their likes and dislikes as they toured the building, Poplak jotting down notes and drawing rough sketches as they went. The basic theme was for the historical rooms – the drawing room, dining room and entrance hall – to maintain an aura of grandeur and stateliness without being too suffocating. The bedrooms, nursery and two studies were to be young, light and airy. Then they left him to it as they organized their wedding at St Paul's Cathedral and honeymoon on board the Royal Yacht *Britannia* in the Mediterranean. While they enjoyed their new life together, the couple kept in close touch with Poplak. Diana slipped away from Balmoral, where the couple prolonged their honeymoon, to view the Aladdin's cave of wedding gifts and decide where to place the various objects. Some, such as the thirty pairs of plain white double sheets with matching pillow cases, were immediately useful. Others, such as antlers and canoes, were destined for eternal storage.

The storage of the presents was something of a headache in itself. For a time they were on display in the cinema at Buckingham Palace, before an exodus of vans and trucks transferred many of them to Kensington Palace. There they were stored in empty rooms and in the disused chapel, which is used as a communal junk store. Their gifts were placed alongside Lord Snowdon's photographic gear and two huge elephant tusks once given to Princess Alice, Countess of Athlone. The influx of so many bulky presents forced a clear-out of the chapel. During the giant spring-clean a superb collection of silk firescreens were discovered, labelled 'Property of HM Queen'. They were owned by the Queen Mother and had been there for more than thirty years. The Queen Mother was quick to have this find brought to her London home, Clarence

House. Then she proudly invited Princess Margaret to lunch, to view this unexpected treasure trove. The Princess examined the firescreens, which had been stored literally next door to her for all those years, and silkily suggested that her mother might like to go upstairs for an afternoon nap. The wily old lady, realizing that she might end up missing several screens, would not be moved. 'No darling,' she replied. 'Why don't you go for a lie down instead?' The Princess left empty handed.

During the redecorating, which took eighteen months, Poplak or an assistant would go around to the chapel to retrieve another item the couple had chosen. The royal couple, who were living at Buckingham Palace, regularly inspected the work and approved outline sketches for future rooms. Just as often, however, they altered them – at the last minute Diana added a second bathroom off the master bedroom. Despairingly she told one friend: 'I've changed my mind six times on one room and it's still not right.'

The grand staircase was painted white, then stripped back to the original wood and finally a compromise was reached. The rails were painted, the handrail left in its original state. There was some resentment in the high-class decorating trade that so many master craftsmen were tied up on the project. It was holding up work for other clients. It wasn't until 1982, when Diana was expecting Prince William, that the apartment was ready for occupation. Highgrove was ready several months earlier.

In spite of the temporary setbacks the Princess grew very fond of Mr Poplak and came to rely on his guidance on the colour schemes for her own wardrobe. While she had the advice of Anna Harvey, the deputy fashion editor of *Vogue*, her choice of colours was influenced by Poplak's own colour 'signature' – he prefers puces, dark blues, aubergines, and pastel shades. 'He made her feel comfortable and secure,' recalls one colleague. Such was the friendship between the royal couple and their designer that when he broke a leg during a skiing accident in Switzerland, they frequently phoned him to check on his condition and also sent flowers and handwritten notes. He has become a regular dinner party guest and still works for the couple.

What is the feeling of the house created for Diana and Charles? Poplak's critics say it is too blandly tasteful, rather like a high-class Chicago hotel. However, most visitors are impressed by the light and airy style, the combination of pastel colours offsetting formal period furniture and gilt-framed oil paintings. Over-all it has the feeling of a home rather than a palace.

For the other residents of this royal village, the arrival of the Prince and Princess of Wales sent ripples through their placid existence. Security was strengthened and with that the friendly easygoing atmosphere disappeared. No one was more affected than Prince and Princess Michael of Kent. Security experts ordered that a beautiful pair of wrought iron gates at the bottom of their garden should be taken down and the wall bricked up to stop possible intruders. The Princess was horrified and bombarded the men from the Ministry with a barrage of letters. Her campaign was in vain. The gates came down, the wall went up. The Princess was heartbroken. A friend who visited on 'demolition day' recalls 'The Princess spoke about their loss more in sorrow than in anger. She felt it was an act of wanton vandalism. The Wales's weren't blamed directly for the decision but it did not help relations.'

Besides the Michaels, their near neighbours included the Duke and Duchess of Beaufort, while down the drive in the Old Barracks live Diana's sister Jane and her husband, Robert Fellowes, the Queen's deputy private secretary. Charles's cousin-in-law, the artist Robert Van Eyck, lives in the Upper Stable, while from her sitting room window Diana looks over the Wren House, now occupied by the Queen's former private secretary, Sir Philip Moore, and the white-painted Nottingham Cottage which was built with spare bricks from the palace and was once occupied by the notorious Marion Crawford, governess to the Queen and Princess Margaret, who sold her memoirs.

A visitor invited to look around Diana's London home has to be cleared by the now ubiquitous Royal Protection Squad. First he is stopped at the security barrier to have his credentials checked, and then a telephone call is made to the palace to confirm the appointment. The visitor passes the Gloucesters'

apartment and Police Lodge where a bank of television screens
monitor every movement. Turning right, the visitor is confronted by a gravel courtyard with a grassy roundabout in the
middle, decked with shrubs and geraniums. The area is lit by
old fashioned black gas lamps with a red and gold crown on
top. But here the Victorian image ends. As the visitor
crunches over the gravel towards the cream porticoed
entrance, his every movement is watched by the unblinking
stare of a spy camera and two policemen in a sentry box.

The black-painted front door is opened by the couple's
butler, Harold Brown, a quiet, diffident soul who collects
ancient royal photographs. Diana loves to browse through the
extensive collection, which he has built up since he was a boy.
Once in the entrance hall the guest cannot possibly have any
doubt about whose house he is in. An expanse of green and
grey carpet, patterned with the Prince of Wales feathers,
covers the hall and waiting room. It didn't impress Bob
Geldof, the genius behind Live Aid, when he came to discuss
famine relief in Africa with Prince Charles. 'Don't think much
of the carpet,' said the blunt Irishman. Charles agreed. 'It is
rather garish isn't it.'

On the left is an antique table with a leatherbound guest
book. The first signature, dated 20 May 1982, is signed
'Spencer (daddy)'. Others include that of opera singer Kiri Te
Kanawa, Australian Prime Minister Bob Hawke and King
Hussein of Jordan. There are vases of flowers in the alcoves,
giving the visitor an impression of warmth and welcome. The
£40,000 cutglass vase which President and Nancy Reagan gave
the couple as a wedding present is displayed on its own table at
the end of the hallway. Like Princess Margaret, Charles
appreciates glassware. In the equerry's room, off the waiting
room, is a collection he has built up over the years. Other
pieces are dotted about the apartment, but all are displayed out
of the reach of Prince William and Prince Harry.

The Wales's staff, who have their own tradesman's entrance
at the back, are allocated a separate wing to the right of the
lobby. On the ground floor is the laundry room, the wine
cellar, freezer store and staff dining room. At one time they
enjoyed a staff sitting room. However because Diana has so

many clothes that her own extensive walk-in wardrobes cannot cope, this has been converted into a royal clothes store. Her clothes are carefully labelled, colour coded, covered in cellophane and put away by her two dressers, hockey-playing Evelyn Dagley, and Fay Marshalsea. The Princess has eased her space crisis by lending various outfits to some of her friends, and to her sisters Jane and Sarah.

But visitors never get the chance to see the staff quarters because they are ushered through into the waiting hall. Here they can browse through various magazines of the doctor's waiting room variety or catch up with the news in *The Times* and the *Daily Telegraph*. Before being taken up the impressive staircase the visitor might have time to peek into the downstairs loos. These certainly give the outsider an impression of the master of the house. The men's cloakroom is covered with framed certificates showing the Prince's more obscure honours, together with a life-size cartoon of a polo stick poking out of the loo.

In the lavatory itself Charles has given free rein to his sense of humour, displaying the original drawings of newspaper cartoonists such as Giles and Caldwell. In both Kensington Palace and Highgrove the Prince has his Throne Rooms – for his collection of old lavatories. These all have the old wide mahogany seats with chain flush and brass pipes. The bowls are white ceramic with a delicate blue floral pattern. The Prince has gone so deeply into the subject that in his library he has several books on old loos and where to find them.

As the visitor walks up the broad staircase, among the many gilt framed oil paintings (mostly on loan from the Queen's priceless collection) one picture stands out. It is a four foot high painting of Princess Diana in her famous Emanuel wedding dress. It was commissioned by a delighted Prince Charles when Diana told him that he would be a father for the second time. Artist John Ward did the first of three sittings in the drawing room, on the day that Buckingham Palace announced that the Princess was expecting – appropriately St Valentine's Day, 1984.

Arriving at the first floor the visitor finds the Princess's sitting room, the large drawing room (which can hold sixty for a reception), Prince Charles's study, the dining room, and, in the staff wing, the German-designed kitchen, breakfast room and various glass and silver pantries.

The Princess's north facing sitting room is sadly in shade most of the day but she has a quaint view of the royal village, looking out over the gravel courtyard and the white-painted cottages with scented roses growing up the walls. Again the Prince of Wales feathers are the motif of the dusky pink and blue trellised wallpaper, a theme continued in the cushions. From the pink four-seater sofa the Princess watches the television; her sitting room is the only place in the apartment with one. Diana is a regular viewer of *Eastenders*, *Dallas* and *Dynasty*. She thinks that actor Leslie Grantham, who plays the notorious Dirty Den in *Eastenders*, is a 'lovable rogue'. If the Princess is out for the evening a member of staff will video her favourite soap operas. She also has an extensive collection of video films – she particularly enjoyed *Amadeus*, the film about the tragic life of Mozart.

In her sitting room are mementoes of her schooldays – a tuck box with 'D. Spencer' stencilled on the side is on the windowsill. Her antismoking views are made clear by the stark No Smoking sign on the grey marble fireplace. In her four-tiered bookcase she has hardback books covering a wide number of interests: gardening, New Zealand, sewing and knitting, as well as the usual classics. Next to the sofa she has displayed her collection of Crummle boxes; one sweet little china box, a gift from her husband, says simply 'With love, Charles', and is decorated with hearts. Another gift from Charles is the jolly Wemyes pig which he bought for her for Christmas 1986. Photographs of the family in gilt and silver frames adorn every available surface. Snapshots of William in his Parachute Regiment red beret, Prince Harry in his blue dungarees, Charles, Edward and Andrew on the verandah deck of the Royal Yacht *Britannia* during a cruise of the Western Isles.

On Diana's desk are her pictures of Highgrove and Prince Charles asleep in a chair. Tucked away in her desk drawer is her very private photograph album with pictures that only a few select friends are ever allowed to see. Pictures of Prince

William as a baby in a bouncing cradle being chucked under the chin by his great-grandmother, Lady Fermoy, snapshots of Diana in a grey silk nightdress tucking in to a bowlful of cereal, a miniature packet of Rice Krispies in her hand, and the Princess, wearing a joke plastic bosom, trying, with Prince Andrew's help, to debag Prince Charles during the annual family Christmas gathering at Windsor Castle.

Like Prince Andrew, Princess Diana is a keen photographer who enjoys taking family pictures. When she is away on tour she asks her staff to take regular photographs of William and Harry so that she doesn't miss a day of their development.

Across the landing from Diana's sitting room is Prince Charles's study. It has the air of a don's retreat, not least because the three windows look out on to what appears to be a peaceful college quadrangle, paved and arcaded with sturdy brick columns. Curiously, this has been known for centuries as Prince of Wales Court. The Prince was Frederick, the cello-playing son of George II and father of George III. His sister, Princess Anne, played the clavichord, with no less than the composer Handel as her master of music. In this cloistered courtyard there were French dances in the open air for royal birthdays and other events.

Tucked away in an alcove is a now rather lonely kennel, which formerly housed Prince Charles's much loved golden labrador Harvey. He used to accompany the Prince on his long fishing trips, but after the dog developed arthritis in his back legs he just couldn't keep up. Harvey was looked after by Charles's former chef, Graham Newbold, and the dog made his home in the first floor kitchen. Finally the day came when even climbing up the staff stairs became too much. The Royal Comptroller of the Household, Lieutenant-Colonel Philip Creasey, volunteered to look after the family pet. On the day he took him to his home in Kent, the staff came out to wave goodbye. 'It was all quite touching,' said one servant.

The Prince's study reflects the air of studious quiet in the courtyard. His bookcase – the original Georgian which had suffered bomb damage, now restored – is full of books by long-forgotten Greek philosophers, the psychoanalyst Carl Jung, Victorian aesthete John Ruskin, the works of novelist

Alexander Solzhenitsyn, and his fellow Russian, the political prisoner Mihajlo Mikhajlov. Their writings on the nature of the relationship between mind and body, art and environment, society and the role of the individual, have formed the building blocks of Charles's own world view.

Closer to home is a copy of Sheila MacCleod's book on anorexia nervosa, the slimmer's disease, kept in Charles's desk drawer. He kept it there under lock and key and referred to it often in the agonising months after the birth of Prince William, when Diana was obsessed about regaining her figure. The Prince knew that her elder sister, Sarah, had suffered from the illness and was genuinely worried that Diana was going down the same anguished path.

It is at his desk that Charles writes most of his speeches and where he keeps in touch with his closest advisers. He has a space-age telephone with a screen, on which he can see who he is talking to when the other person has a similar system. His friend, the American oil magnate Dr Armand Hammer, the Duke of Westminster and Prince Philip have their own screens and communicate in this way. It was on this system that the royal family held a threeway conference between Balmoral, Buckingham Palace and Kensington Palace in the summer of 1985 during the crisis over Princess Michael's seven-year marriage. At that time she was going through her pink wig period; she was seen by newspaper reporters coming out of a Belgravia flat very early one morning with her friend, Texan property tycoon, John Ward Hunt, wearing a wig disguise. The resulting stories prompted a family summit where it was decided that the family should rally round the beleagured Michaels.

Like Diana, Charles keeps mementoes of the family everywhere in his room. Pictures of the Queen Mother, the Queen and Lord Mountbatten adorn the walls, while on his desk is a cheekily charming photograph of Prince William holding up his kilt and showing off his pants. Next to it is a snapshot of Charles with his father, bearing Charles's inscription 'I was not born to follow in my father's footsteps', a tart reference to his own often stormy relations with Prince Philip and his future constitutional role.

Opposite the window is an alcove which is almost an inner sanctum, where Prince Charles displays two of his most treasured possessions, a wooden block with the flag of the banned Polish trade union Solidarity mounted in it, and a model of the space shuttle *Challenger*. Both reflect qualities of human endeavour and achievement and are tributes to human courage in the face of adversity and repression. It is a subject which fascinates him, as many of his own outside activities bear testimony. 'In the West . . . so much sophistication, so much technology, so much waste has made us blasé and complacent, and unable to see where we ought to draw the line, what we ought to stand up for, what are our real beliefs, when do we say "this far we will go, and no further," what things are really worth fighting for?' As a reminder of his own Action Man days he has a silver model of the Royal Navy's minesweeper, HMS *Bronington*, which he commanded briefly.

It is in this study that he likes to spend time each day in some form of meditation. At one time he tried yoga after his friend, the violinist Yehudi Menuhin, recommended his own tutor.

His study is one of the few rooms in the house – the nursery is the other – where the fire is actually lit rather than decorated with dried flowers. The Prince loves open fires because they remind him of his nursery days with Nanny Mabel Anderson at Buckingham Palace. 'So cozy,' he says. 'Cozy' is a favourite royal word, as is his often used royal expletive 'Oh braces'.

From the two most personal rooms on the first floor the visitor moves to the drawing and dining rooms, where Dudley Poplak incorporated many of the formal wedding gifts against a background of mustard flock wallpaper with a deep yellow border. A magnificent £7000 Broadwood grand piano, also a wedding present, dominates the drawing room. Diana admits that she 'fiddles around on it' but she is doing her talent a disservice. At a concert she was observed 'playing' along with her fingers during a rendition of Greig's piano concerto in A minor, one of her favourite piano pieces.

At the other end of the drawing room there is a Flemish tapestry depicting a harvest scene. It was here that the royal couple sat for their famous television interview with Sir Alastair Burnet. It is also where Prince Charles conducts morning audiences with guests, who range from the Indian Prime Minister Rajiv Gandhi and Paul Boateng, the controversial London councillor, to officials from his various charities and new commanding officers of regiments of which he is colonel-in-chief. Once more family portraits abound, but in keeping with the tone they are rather more formal: Charles in his Naval dress uniform, Princess Margaret in her tiara. Quaintly, she pronounces it 'terrarra' and says that only the Queen can put her tiara on while walking downstairs.

The dining room, dominated by a polished round table, is elegant, rather grand, and quite capable of taking sixteen at a sitting. In the staff wing is the fitted kitchen, again, a wedding present. The couple were given so many that, unknown to the manufacturer, one was cut down and used in the nursery. The first kitchen, complete with double-drainer sink, dishwasher and fitted units, was replaced by a German make during Christmas 1986.

Retracing the route from the kitchen, through the drawing room and back on to the landing, the visitor turns right past a lift – which carries the household supplies – to the royal couple's bedroom. This wing of the apartment houses the sleeping quarters, and, on the floor above, the royal nursery. It was in the master bedroom that the Princess made last minute design changes, incorporating a second mirrored and marbled bathroom into the plan. Now both have huge walk-in wardrobes, separate bathrooms – Diana's is the only one with a bidet – and their own dressing rooms. Before she moved some of her clothes downstairs, Charles complained that she was trespassing on his wardrobe space.

The Prince, who has his own door to the bedroom, will often sleep in the single bed in his dressing room if he has a late night or a very early start the following day. They both need their rest – although the maids used to complain at the extra work involved.

The master bedroom is dominated by a 7 ft 6 in-wide oak fourposter bed. Diana's side of the mattress has been resprung to give her firmer support while she sleeps. The Princess suffers from back trouble, a legacy of having picked up William and Harry taking their weight on her back rather

Prince Charles and Princess Diana in their drawing room at
Kensington Palace

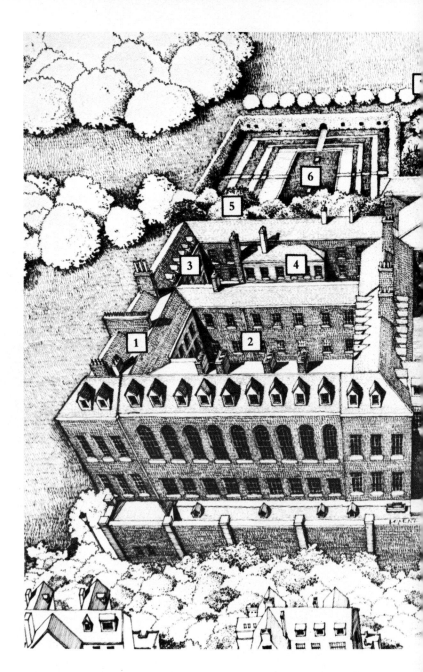

Illustration of Kensington Palace, showing the location of the various royal households

Above: Princess Diana in her study, which overlooks the courtyard at the entrance to her home

Left: While still a toddler, Prince William had an important meeting with the press in his parents' walled garden

Above: Prince William
and his mother in the
day nursery

Right: Off on another
royal engagement.
Princess Diana boards
a helicopter in Perk's
Field, which forms
part of Kensington
Gardens

Fashion workshop with the Emanuels at Kensington Palace.
Princess Diana's working clothes make an important contribution
to her public image

Above: A private lunch with Lady Dale 'Kanga' Tryon at a Knightsbridge restaurant
Below: That looks like fun: Princess Diana crowned her husband with a fake glass bottle during a tour of the James Bond set at Pinewood Studios

Very much in the public eye on a private night out on the town, Princess Diana, in black leather skirt and lace tights, shivers in freezing temperatures as she leaves a West End theatre

than her legs. As a result, a private Harley Street physiotherapist regularly calls at Kensington Palace to give her lumbar massage and exercise. On top of their bed is the curious sight of an array of cuddly toys. On Charles's side is a bald shabby teddy bear that the Prince takes everywhere with him. Each night it is tucked up by his valet, Ken Stronach, and waits there patiently for Charles. Teddy, a friend from childhood, even travels overseas with the Prince. It is carried with the rest of his luggage in a shirt bag and put into his bed at night. The only occasion when he leaves teddy at home is when the Prince, as Colonel-in-Chief, visits his regiments. He feels that it would be unbecoming for his bedtime secret to be discovered by the elite fighting troops he represents.

Princess Diana too has her own toy friends to cuddle up to at night. She collects frogs – a reminder of a private joke between the royal couple about the fairy story of the Prince who kissed a frog and it turned into a Princess. She prefers grey silk nighties to sleep in, and lounges around the apartment in a red cotton dressing gown in the morning. Charles sleeps in blue silk pyjamas and has a tatty dressing gown, decorated with Prince of Wales feathers, which he refuses to part with. It has been sewn back together so often that it is a miracle it stays in one piece.

Off the master bedroom is Diana's dressing room. It is functional, with none of the Hollywood-style glamour normally associated with a star's dressing room. The decoration in the room is simple, with a cream carpet, kidney-shaped dressing table, several chests of drawers, and floor length mirrors. From time to time Diana will use this room to try on new outfits brought to her by her regular designers. When she goes through these impromptu fashion shows she displays all the professionalism of a model, stripping down to her bra and panties in front of hovering assistants. 'It is quite a surprising sight to see a girl who is on the cover of every magazine virtually starkers,' said one dressmaker.

Next to her dressing room is a small sewing room where her dressers will perform running repairs on her outfits and press them so that they are neat and crisp before the Princess embarks on a public engagement.

The Prince is rather more formal. He has his own quaintly named 'brushing room' where his valet lays out his clothes, helps him dress and puts a final polish to his shoes before he leaves. The daily spit and polish is performed by an Army orderly, normally from the Ghurkas, who cleans the Prince's handmade shoes each night.

Above the royal couple on the next floor is the nursery for William and Harry. Although the Prince and Princess are both early risers they are often disturbed by a thump, thump, thump, as William begins his morning playtime with his baby brother. The nursery is divided into two: the day nursery for play; the night nursery where the children share a room. William takes a toy parrot to bed with him. They have their own bathroom with children-size toilets and washbasin. Further along the corridor Nanny Ruth Wallace has her own bedsitting room, with a bathroom en suite.

From the day nursery the children can look out from the attic windows – barred for safety – to the paddock where the royal helicopters take off. William in particular is fascinated by these machines. He imitates the arm signals of the ground crew and knows the names of most of the Queen's flight pilots; one of the first words he learned was 'plane'. The nursery, like the rest of the house, is neat, clean and tidy, reflecting the fastidious nature of the mistress of the household. Diana chose Beatrix Potter crockery and paintings for the children. The boys have the usual toys, Fisher Price rings, jigsaws, inflatable green frogs, and toy cars, together with some of Charles's nursery toys which he rescued from the basement of Buckingham Palace. William has a troop of foot-high toy soldiers in his nursery window, drilled in perfect marching order. Harry learned to walk using Jumbo, Charles's old wheeled elephant. They also have a rocking horse given to them by Nancy Reagan when she made a lunchtime visit.

Walking from the nursery back to the main staircase the visitor comes across two guest bedrooms, one for overnight stays, the second rather more substantial. They are used mainly by Diana's ladies-in-waiting. Her senior lady-in-waiting, Anne Beckwith-Smith, may drive from her

Wiltshire home to stay in London for the night if there is an early morning engagement.

Prior to her marriage, the Duchess of York took refuge here at the height of the speculation about her plans to marry Prince Andrew. Charles's cousins from Liechtenstein, Prince Hans Adam and Princess Marie, with whom the couple go skiing, have also stayed. Laurens van der Post, Charles's intellectual guru, will sometimes stay the night when he is in London. It is on this floor that the staff have their quarters, bedrooms with dreamy dormer windows neatly ensconced in the cottage attics. A Scotland Yard protection officer sleeps here, as well as the couple's New Zealand born cook, their valet, butler, the housekeeper, maid, and dresser.

At the top of the residence, on the flat roof, is the royal couple's pride and joy and a source of irritation to the other royal residents. It is their railed roof garden, complete with greenhouse and barbeque, where on balmy summer evenings Charles loves to cook salmon steaks, corn on the cob and jacket potatoes in foil for the family. Here the Princess sunbathes topless, well away from the public gaze, and the couple grow clematis and miniature tomatoes from seed.

Not since the days of Queen Caroline has the royal family produced a royal couple who are so interested in gardening. 'It is my particular eccentricity,' admits Prince Charles when he talks about the old-fashioned vegetables such as red cabbage which he tries to grow.

However their secluded roof garden has not pleased everyone. Princess Margaret has moaned privately that they don't use it frequently enough, while Princess Michael, allocated the smallest royal residence, fumes that she doesn't have one of her own. But she was not to be defeated. She invited the former Minister for the Environment, Michael Heseltine, to dinner. She bemoaned the lack of space for her children, Lord Freddie and Lady Ella, and suggested it would be marvelous if they could have a roof terrace like the Prince and Princess of Wales. Heseltine, who was new to the job, didn't realise that they already had a garden. (As soon as Princess Alice, Countess of Athlone died, there was a swift exchange of memoes between Princess Michael and the Property Service Agency, and after some wrangling she was given Alice's garden.) So he reluctantly agreed to pay for a roof garden. But even in the royal outdoors there is a certain pecking order. The Michaels' piece of SW Heaven clings to the side of the house, has plastic grass flooring and space enough only for two beach chairs and a table. It also annoys Diana because it overlooks her bedroom. The ultimate irony is that Princess Michael considers it too dangerous for the children to play in, so they have to make do with their ground level garden.

Diana and Charles, who came in for criticism for allowing the daisies to overrun their own walled-in garden, let their children run free here. There is a swing, slide and a couple of sturdy park benches. In the summer Charles and Diana like to take tea in the garden, writing letters to friends and family, listening to their personal stereos or quietly reading a book. To keep in touch with the outside world Charles takes his portable telephone along with him.

It was during one such tea party that the famous row between Prince Charles and Princess Michael erupted. Prince Charles had asked his butler, Allan Fisher, to take a tray out for afternoon tea. Fisher, a flamboyant character who had formerly worked for the Windsors in Paris and for Bing Crosby, did as he was bidden. As he was taking the tray into the garden he realized that he had forgotten something. He swore loudly, a shade too loudly for Princess Michael who was upstairs in her bedroom having an afternoon nap. She appeared at her open window and shouted down 'Don't use that kind of language here, don't you realise there are children about?'

Fisher would not be spoken to in this manner. He turned on his heels and went inside to complain to Prince Charles. Like mothers and their children, the royal family are very proprietorial about their staff. Charles flared. He marched around to the Princess's front door and hammered on the knocker. It was opened by the butler who was told that the Prince wanted to see Princess Michael *immediately*. The Princess appeared. 'If you have any complaints about my staff speak to me about them first,' he told her. Then he walked off, leaving the Princess, for once, speechless.

Indeed, all is not peace and tranquility in the garden. Prince Charles's passion for improvements caused problems with other less regal residents. He decided to install two miniature fountains and cut down a tree to accommodate them. During his tour of Italy in 1985 he constantly called Kensington Palace to see how the building work was progressing. When he arrived home he was delighted to find the fountains installed and working. His elderly neighbours were not so impressed. One tenant moaned 'The sound of all that running water makes me want to go to the loo all day.' Eventually he wrote to the Prince to complain.

This then is the village where the Prince and Princess of Wales have made their London home. It was a labour of love to create, and their arrival drastically upset the pedestrian pace of the palace. However the real beauty of the place for Diana and Charles is that it allows them a haven where they can lead secret and essentially separate lives, away from the constant click of cameras.

Behind the red brick walls of Kensington Palace the real characters of Diana and Charles come into focus – and the picture is rather different from the public image.

3

The Private Life of
the Prince and Princess
of Wales

Like an overweight dragonfly, the squat shadow of a shiny red helicopter looms large on the London skyline, the clatter of its rotor blades shattering the lazy hum of a hot summer's afternoon.

As the Wessex of the Queen's Flight slowly descends with pin point accuracy on to a wide 'H' in a grassy paddock, two small boys rush to the window of their nursery. 'Mummy's home, mummy's home,' they chorus excitedly. The mummy in question is Princess Diana, home to Kensington Palace after another day taking centre stage in the eternal royal roadshow.

Minutes later as she crunches towards the entrance of Apartments 8 and 9, butler Harold Brown opens the door to allow Prince William and Prince Harry to race towards her. Sometimes as a treat they will be allowed to go to Perk's Field to watch the helicopter land. As the afternoon's shadows lengthen it is now time to play; the Princess and her two boys go to her sitting room to watch *Blue Peter* on television – 'The one sure way of keeping William quiet,' says Diana – or up to the nursery to catch up on the events of the day. For Diana this is a short period in which to relax, to take precious moments away from remorseless public scrutiny. In the five years that she and Prince Charles have called Kensington Palace their home Diana has come to regard it as a private sanctuary, a place where she can lead a life she can call her own and develop a style that only the privileged few know about.

Behind the front door of her Kensington Palace apartment a very different Diana emerges from her cocoon, a lively and flighty social butterfly, a world away from the public image of a demure Princess dressed in dowdy middle-aged fashions, smiling sweetly and asking polite questions.

During her short life she has been described in many different ways, but many of the easy images like 'shy Di' merely hinder rather than help an understanding of this international royal star. One recent biographer, Suzanne Lowry, says the Princess is 'truly an enigma' who has become 'middle aged, staid and matronly'. Others say that she is a steely tyrant who dominates her henpecked husband. Yet more vow that she is charming and witty, others that she is dim but delightful. The contradictions add to the enigma and the public become all the more confused. The difficulty lies between her public and private life. While it is said that the royal family live their lives in a goldfish bowl, constantly on view, the reality is that it is a goldfish bowl where most of the glass is opaque.

When they are on duty – undertaking a public engagement or on an overseas tour – the royal family put on a performance. During these performances they may give a glimpse of their character, but no more than any actor does while on stage. Is Meryl Streep, for instance, really like the lost and lonely woman she played in the film *The French Lieutenant's Woman*? Of course not. So why should Princess Diana in her private life be a mirror image of her public persona?

Like many public personalities the royal family create an image – or it is created for them – and they hide their real personalities behind it. At home, when the barriers are up and their guard is down, they take off their masks and show their real faces. Yet the world cannot see into this goldfish bowl of red brick.

When Diana arrives home the transformation is almost immediate. She will often literally kick off her shoes and skip down the entrance hall, before going up to her dressing room to change into a trendy outfit from her extensive private wardrobe. The days when she would arrive home and slump, totally drained, against the front door or sit silently in a chair, are now gone.

Staff smile at the image of her wearing matronly fashions. Her working clothes – when she worries about the wind, children looking up her skirt and flying the flag – are far removed from her private outfits. At home she wears slinky satin trousers, sexy leather skirts and sensual silk blouses. Italian designers such as Valentino and Gianna Versace are favoured. Prince Charles approves. 'I like my wife in Italian clothes, I think they suit her very well.' At the same time she is certainly a home maker who enjoys the simple pleasures of family life. But there is more to her than a one dimensional caricature of the winsome wife and mother.

Diana is considerate and chummy with her staff yet shows the Spencer steel and aristocratic arrogance with those who do not match her exacting standards. At home she is obsessional about neatness and perfection – all her shoes have to be placed in an exact order in her wardrobes. She is independent and aloof – her relationship with the Queen is cool and formal – yet something of an exhibitionist who enjoys flirting. She enjoys swimming in the nude, loved dancing on stage at Covent Garden and likes to use her sweetly coquettish charms at dinner parties. Her life with Charles is governed by the iron laws of royal timetables; brief chats in the morning, sometimes lunch together, occasionally dinner. Often as not when he hosts a dinner she will go out on her own to see a show or dine with friends. These days Diana is an Uptown Girl who enjoys the nightlife London has to offer.

Behind the closed doors of Kensington Palace the couple enjoy a sparky marriage. A 'rumbustious' relationship where a sloppy kiss and a bearhug will follow a battle of wills. Diana's rows with Charles are spectacular and short lived, like dog fights during the Battle of Britain. She rarely emerges the victor. As one courtier says: 'When Charles is angry he is a very, very formidable character.' The royal couple are aristocrats who have been brought up in hard social schools – but with Prince Philip as his exacting headmaster, Charles has had the tougher education.

While Diana has changed Charles's wardrobe, Charles has moulded Diana's character. Before her marriage and during their engagement she was a determined meat and two veg girl who tucked in to her Beef Wellington with the rest. When he went vegetarian, overnight the Princess followed suit. He did it out of philosophical conviction, but she did it to please him.

Ever since Diana first came to live at Kensington Palace her life has been dominated by learning the royal ropes, shaping her marriage and fitting in the demands of a family with those of a royal life. Naturally she has two distinct regimes: the routine for the days she is working for the Royal Family Firm; and another for the days she is free. Whatever is on the agenda her day starts with a gentle tap on the bedroom door from the butler, who discreetly leaves a tray of freshly-made coffee in the corridor. She slowly sips a cup of weak coffee and then quickly dons her navy blue and yellow tracksuit and heads downstairs. Meanwhile Charles is still surfacing. He is a grumpy early-morning riser who starts the day by listening to the last minutes of the farming programme on Radio 4.

By the side of their bed Charles has a notebook and pen, where he writes down what he can remember of his dreams. The exercise is part of trying to understand the inner self, an approach to life linked to the teachings of psychoanalyst Carl Jung. 'I think one can probably learn a considerable amount from them,' Charles says.

In the courtyard Princess Diana's Ford Escort is waiting. At seven o'clock she unobtrusively joins the early morning traffic and makes the ten minute journey to Buckingham Palace, where she heads for the heated indoor pool. The Princess, a keen swimmer and an expert diver, makes a point of going for a twenty minute dip wherever she is in the world. It is her way of starting the day in the right frame of mind. If she spends the weekend at Windsor Castle she and Princess Margaret go skinny dipping in the glassed-in pool. At Highgrove she switches off the remote control police surveillance camera when she swims nude. The Princess prefers the breaststroke and does between twenty and thirty brisk lengths of the Buckingham Palace pool, arriving back at Kensington Palace with her hair wet but combed. She swims so often that her regular hairdresser, Scotsman Richard Dalton, suggested she change her style to a shorter, sportier length so that it was more manageable; hence the new-look Princess.

When William is on school holidays the Princess takes the boys to Buckingham Palace in the afternoon for a swimming lesson. While Diana continues swimming on her own, Nanny Wallace dries and dresses the boys before they are presented to the Queen. William has a well-deserved reputation as an unholy terror. Once when Diana left him with 'Gary' – his early babytalk for 'Granny' – a secretary came across the Queen chasing her errant grandson down the red-carpeted corridors. 'Don't you smile, young lady,' said the Queen in mock scolding tones. 'This will happen to you one day.'

From time to time Diana will use these dawn runs to fulfill a personal ambition. On one occasion she visited the studios of the BBC's *Breakfast Time* because she wanted to see Selina Scott in action. The Princess, who still gets starstruck, asked the television personality about her job as they enjoyed breakfast together. She performed a similar stunt when she drove to Broadcasting House to watch the Radio 1 disc jockey Mike Smith at work. When her favourite disc jockey, Graham Dene, hosted his last early morning show, the Princess went along to Capital Radio and acted as a secret co-host. She even brought along her favourite records. During the two-and-a-half hour broadcast she sat silently in the studio, sipping tea and eating sticky buns. The only clue given to the listeners was when Dene signed off by playing Diana's favourite record, Billy Joel's 'Uptown Girl', dedicated to 'Charles back at Kensington'.

Normally, however, Diana has an early morning workout on her own and is normally back at Kensington Palace by 7.40 for breakfast at 7.45. As in other royal households, Diana and Charles breakfast separately. Charles does not emerge until about 8.20. This has been taken as a sign that their marriage is crumbling. It is merely that both have different timetables. These are rigidly adhered to and typed out beforehand. Everyone from the private secretary to the cook receives a copy so they can plan their own day. For example, while Diana is out enjoying her swim, her Ghurka orderly is busily setting the table in the dining room for her breakfast.

Like the rest of the family, Diana eats a frugal breakfast. She prefers pink grapefruit sprinkled with health-giving Bemax, or muesli followed by two slices of toast and marmalade and a cup of weak coffee. During her pregnancies she lived off bacon and tomatoes. Normally she eats alone, although when the Duchess of York is in town she often drops in for a girls-only breakfast. In the early days of her marriage Diana was known to walk into the kitchen in her pink cotton dressing gown and wander around barefoot, or in a pair of opentoed slippers, chatting to the off-duty police officers who drop in for a cup of tea. Occasionally she would offer to make them some tea as she bopped around the kitchen listening to the pop music on Capital Radio.

As her postbag has grown and her sense of being royal has developed, her visits to the kitchen have become less frequent. She eats her toast while browsing through the morning mail – opened with one of Charles's prized collection of mother-of-pearl letter openers – and glances through the papers; the *Daily Mail* and *Daily Express* are always delivered.

At the weekend, always spent at Highgrove, the Princess makes a point of reading the downmarket tabloid, the *News of the World*. She either goes down to the kitchen to borrow a copy or asks for it to be brought up to her. If there is something outrageous about her, Harold Brown covers the copy with brown paper for a joke.

Highgrove is the only place where the Wales breakfast as a family; at Kensington Palace William and Harry eat in the nursery. During the week at Kensington Diana's days start in earnest around eight o'clock, when she goes to her dressing room to prepare for the day's royal engagements. Her dressers will have laid out the outfit chosen for the day. When they greet her they curtsey and say: 'Good morning, Your Royal Highness.' Afterwards they address her as 'Ma'am'. This protocol is observed in all the royal households.

As she puts on her makeup – from the Body Shop – her hairdresser blowdries her hair, while the sound of Capital Radio provides a background to their chat. If her timetable allows she always takes Prince William to school – after first going in to kiss Prince Harry goodbye. Since January 1987 William has attended Wetherby preparatory school in nearby Notting Hill. Like the other 120 boys he has to be there at nine o'clock sharp. If Diana cannot take him in the blue Ford Granada estate car, his personal bodyguard deputizes.

When Princess Diana is on duty she is usually briefed about her engagements the day before in her sitting room, by her equerry, Commander Richard Aylard, and her senior lady-in-waiting, Anne Beckwith-Smith. If it is a visit to a Dr Barnardo's centre, for example, she will be given the names and brief details of the principal people she is to meet and the work of the centre. That is if time allows – normally she reads through her background papers the night before or in the car or helicopter on the way to her engagement. Her workload, between four and six engagements a week, is about the same as the average Lady Mayoress's, but rather more glamorous. She always tries to get home by half-past four so that she can play with her children. While she gets her show on the road Charles limbers up for the day ahead in his own way.

While Diana starts her day off with a swim, Charles prefers a good long bath. His valet will run the bath, testing that it is at the correct temperature with a thermometer at the side, and lay out his clothes. After his tub the Prince puts on a dab of Crabtree and Evelyn's West Indian and Sicilian Lime Extract aftershave, a quick squirt of unscented hair lacquer to hold his thinning locks in place, and then gets dressed.

Normally the Prince listens to Radio 4's *Today* show, or else tunes in to Radio 3, depending on his mood. His breakfast at 8.20 is as frugal as Diana's is: fruit, toast and Lapsong Suchong tea sweetened with a dollop of honey. In his bachelor days he didn't drink tea or coffee because of the caffeine content. Like the Duke of Gloucester he stuck to water or milk. After breakfast the Prince likes to read *The Times*, sitting in another relic from his single days, a large cock-fighting chair. The wooden chair, with high arms containing drawers and a table at the back, was once used by bookmakers to take wagers on the fight.

After browsing through the paper and sifting through his mail the Prince gets down to the morning paperwork on his desk. Within the space of an hour he can be dealing with everything from the bathroom heating to the soul of mankind. There are the boxes containing State documents which need to be signed – if the Queen is on tour he takes over her duties – briefing papers to be read and business matters concerning the Duchy of Cornwall to consider.

Prince Charles normally spends an hour in the morning on his administrative duties; unfortunately he does tend to get behind on this chore, especially during the polo season. It is from his desk that he writes his letters. All are handwritten using a black fountain pen. The royal couple are copious letter writers. Charles scatters notes to his valets and butler all over the house. They are left in his pockets, on his bed, discarded on the desk. Some deal with the timetable – who is coming for dinner and when – others are complaints about the running of the household. Contrary to the mild-mannered public image, Prince Charles is a very demanding boss who has exacting standards of service. In an angry mood, he once wrote to one valet 'I didn't mean you to remove that glass for my toothbrush. It was a particularly nice glass. Please bring it back. If they have removed it I shall be very angry indeed. C.'

Underlining for emphasis is a habit. In another note about the maids, writing in a bold felt tip, he complains 'Please ask housemaids not to fiddle with radiators – especially in bathroom, where I had turned radiator off to prevent it becoming like a greenhouse. C.'

While the Princess is technically in charge of running their apartment, Charles takes an active, indeed fussy, interest in its smooth operation. Staff know to keep well out of the way if he is in a temper. Like the rest of his family he will suddenly 'flare'. Once when he returned from a military review he arrived home in a fury. His valet had given him a hat that was too large and he considered that he had been made to look a fool. The royal family take a competitive pride in the way they look at formal military events. Charles stormed down the corridor, unbuckled his silver sword – an heirloom passed down from George V – and hurled it at the wall. The sword sailed over the servant's head, hitting the wall and taking out a lump of plaster. Charles never apologized, but neither was the incident ever alluded to again.

However royal staff do exaggerate the problems. A story, surely apocryphal, in staff circles is that one valet left the

Prince's service when Charles, furious at a misdemeanour, wrapped a thin brass poker around his neck. As one Kensington Palace servant says: 'In this place you can have the sniffles in the morning but by five o'clock you are suffering from double pneumonia.' While the Prince keeps a close eye on domestic matters, he also finds time to write to friends, and to religious, political and industrial leaders. His desire to take Mass with the Pope when he visited the Vatican in 1985 was not a mere whim but the result of a long and detailed correspondence with His Holiness and the Archbishop of Canterbury. Similarly he writes directly to government ministers about some problem he has noted during a royal visit. 'He does a lot behind the scenes which no one ever knows about,' says one aide.

It is no coincidence that he has his own industrial advisor, Rupert Fairfax, seconded from the Hanson Trust conglomerate. He frequently lunches with leading industrialists such as Alan Sugar, the head of Amstrad, to keep his finger on the pulse of the commercial world, particularly the high-tech manufacturing industry which he sees as Britain's future industrial base.

At ten o'clock the Prince has his daily meeting with his private secretary, currently Sir John Riddell, or his assistant. They will discuss his future programme – 'I hate planning my life so far in advance,' the Prince is fond of moaning – and the week's business. He will also go over the draft of any speech written for him by his advisors. Sometimes three or four drafts of the same speech will be written before Charles is happy with it. Then when he stands up he is likely to discard his notes and speak off the cuff. These days he is very much influenced by his intellectual mentor, the philosopher and explorer Sir Laurens van der Post. One morning when Charles was due to make a speech his entire household was thrown into confusion because the draft sent by van der Post had not arrived. Charles said that he could not speak without it. In fact it was discovered at the last minute that the speech had arrived but had not been delivered to his front door. 'Prince Charles completely panicked,' said a member of staff. The Prince's debt to van der Post is unmistakable. In a television documentary Sir Laurens made on the bushmen of the Kalahari desert he explained how by studying the diversity of nature, the bushmen gradually became aware of the diversity of their own nature. 'It seemed as if nature was for them a mirror, where they learned to recognize and understand aspects of themselves.'

Compare that with the Prince's controversial speech in Canada in 1986. 'I feel that deep in the soul of mankind there is a reflection of the beauty and harmony of the universe. Through the outer manifestation of that reflection we can attain the kind of peace for which we yearn.' The difference is minimal.

In the summer, even philosophical reflections are left for another day. Prince Charles's passion in life is polo. He plays between three and four times a week, and practises equally as often. He will regularly leave a note for his valet saying 'Knocking about, 10.00 sharp' which is his shorthand for saying that he wants his polo gear laid out for when he goes to practise at the polo field near Windsor Castle. He also has a wooden horse at Windsor where he rehearses his stroke play. Before he leaves for an afternoon game – he played on the day Prince Harry was born – he kisses goodbye to Diana and adds 'I will try and score for you and the boys, darling.'

Charles appears for breakfast in his polo trousers and leather boots before driving off in his ancient blue Aston Martin. Such is his obsession for the sport that it is no coincidence that his polo manager, Major Ronald Ferguson, the father of the Duchess of York, sits next to Charles's private secretary at the summer planning meetings at Kensington Palace. 'Everything is geared to his polo,' says an aide. 'The rest fits in around it.' An indication of his interest is shown by the fact that in their early days at Kensington Palace, when they entertained infrequently, they hosted a dinner for their polo playing friends.

In the winter the Prince spends most of his time on the affairs of the nation – even if the nation doesn't notice. 'People think I do nothing,' he says. 'It's just that they don't know what I do.'

An essential part of the Prince's daily routine is his morning audiences with key political and social figures. These take place after his morning meeting with his private secretary and his administrative work. They range from discussions with officials from Operation Raleigh, an adventure programme for young people, to mini summits about world affairs with leaders such as Australia's Prime Minister Bob Hawke. Often these discussions will spill over into lunch time when they may be joined by their respective entourages.

Surprisingly, Prince Charles sees a large number of leaders of *èmigrè* groups living in London, hence his interest in the work of the outlawed Polish trade union Solidarity. Lithuanians, Czechs, Slovaks, all see the Prince as a patron of lost causes. However it is not just the people who desire his attention who he sees. The Prince is also always curious to meet the names who make headlines.

Prince Charles regularly keeps visitors waiting as he plays with his children, and often William will interrupt during an interview and pointedly ask his father what he is doing. Bob Geldof experienced the young Prince's forthright personality when he visited Charles to discuss famine relief projects in Africa. Diana, who is in awe of Geldof's achievements, was horrified when William told the unkempt pop singer that his hair was dirty and needed washing. 'It was so embarrassing,' she said afterwards. 'I could have died.'

Geldof recalls the incident in his autobiography, *Is That It?*. 'Prince William came in and wanted his father to go and play with him. He said he couldn't, he had to talk to this man, indicating me.

"Why do you have to talk to that man?" said the young Prince.

"Because we have work to do," said his father.

"He's all dirty," said the boy.

"Shut up you horrible boy," I said. I was wearing my jeans and sneakers, as usual, and I had my normal five o'clock shadow.

"He's got scruffy hair and wet shoes," said the boy, indicating my beloved and comfortable, but admittedly scuffed suede yellow green sneakers.

"Don't be rude, run along and play" said the now mortified father.

"Your hair's scruffy too," I retorted, to the boy who would be king.

"No it's not, my mummy brushed it," answered my tormentor before leaving the room.'

The story is one that the Prince and Princess also enjoy telling about their son; although embarrassed by his behaviour they are rather proud that he is so self-confident.

Such are the rigours of the timetable that even if both Charles and Diana are at home during the day they will only see each other in passing. She will never just drop in when Charles is meeting visitors, and so they often come away with the impression that she is not at home. That is not the case. She is often to be found in her sitting room or playing with the boys in their nursery. When the Princess is not on parade she leads a very different, very secret private life.

If you were lucky you might catch a glimpse of her dressed in a casual pair of jeans and headscarf heading for the local Sainsburys on nearby Cromwell Road, or slipping unnoticed into a dance studio in Covent Garden to watch a ballet rehearsal. She has even been seen driving around town in a borrowed and very battered green Spitfire sports car so that she can travel totally incognito. Her normal off-duty daily pattern is to spend the morning on royal business, lunch with friends, the afternoons shopping, exercising or gardening, and the evenings out on the town.

The first visitors of the day are her equerry and lady-in-waiting who discuss future engagements, last minute requests and overseas tours. Her diary is always meshed with Prince Charles's. Even though the Princess may be the bigger draw, his engagements take first priority. Diana fits in.

Other morning visitors can include officials from her charities to discuss a pet project, and her dress designers. Couturiers such as Bruce Oldfield, Gina Fratini and Bill Campbell bring along their sketches and samples for royal approval. The queue of designers selling their wares is always longest when the Princess is preparing for a tour. If she is having lunch at home she usually invites a girl friend to join her around one o'clock. Over a light meal in the dining room she likes to catch up on all the latest gossip; this is a lunchtime pattern common to all the royal ladies living in Kensington Palace. During her bachelor days Sarah Ferguson arrived every Thursday for lunch or afternoon tea, and other frequent visitors include Penny Romsey, Diana's gingerhaired sister Jane, Carolyn Warren, the daughter of the Queen's racing manager Lord Porchester, Princess Margaret's daughter Lady Sarah Armstrong-Jones, and Catherine Soames, wife of the Conservative Member of Parliament Nicholas Soames.

Each Monday Diana will be given a printed card, on which her chef, Mervyn Wycherley, offers a number of choices for the week's menus. She picks what is required, pencilling in the number of guests expected for lunch and dinner. Cooking for Diana and Charles is undemanding as their tastes are simple. Salads are a must, jacket potatoes a real favourite. While both are essentially vegetarian they do eat fish and a little chicken. Charles for example loves scrambled eggs with smoked salmon. The following is a menu Diana chose for one week in the summer that is typical of the rest:

Saturday lunch: Croquettes, baked potatoes, crème brûlée

Sunday evening: Tomato mousse, eggs Florentine, summer pudding

Monday lunch: Macaroni cheese, baked potatoes, tarte tatin

Monday dinner: Spinach quiche, apple sorbet

Tuesday lunch: Fish, bearnaise sauce, crème caramel

Tuesday dinner: Oeufs en tartelettes, spaghetti, ice cream, fresh fruit salad

Wednesday lunch: Chicken hollandaise, baked potatoes

Wednesday dinner: Public Engagement

Thursday lunch: Carrot soup, scallops in sauce, spinach soufflé

Thursday dinner: Public Engagement

Friday lunch: Prawn mayonnaise, boiled eggs, salad and baked potatoes, rhubarb

The crème caramel for Tuesday lunch was for Sarah Armstrong-Jones. Diana rarely eats dessert, although she will often have a Kit Kat in the afternoon to keep her going.

Prince Charles is the motivating force behind the move to vegetarianism. 'Light meals make a great difference to one's survival chances. In India it was a joy for me at luncheons and dinners, they always had vegetarian dishes as well. You could choose what you wanted – eminently civilized.'

All their vegetables come from the garden at Highgrove, where the Prince likes to experiment with cold soups. Nettle and lovage soups have been on the menu. His passion for boiled vegetables does not please all their guests. Society writer David Litchfield commented acidly on one Kensington Palace supper party: 'I don't know about dinner with Princess Michael of Kent, dinner with Big Ears doesn't sound like a gastronomic experience worth writing home about.'

Diana does not eat at home all the time however. She has a clutch of favourite restaurants where she meets her friends. The restaurant in the department store Harvey Nichols is a regular haunt, as are high class Knightsbridge eateries such as Ménage à Trois and San Lorenzo. Then it is off for a little shopping, a chance to catch up on what is in and what is out, to buy presents for friends, clothes for the children and sometimes for Prince Charles – but usually only as a treat. Her kingdom is bounded by the royal triangle of Harvey Nichols, the General Trading Company and the fashion stores of Beauchamp Place. She has an account at most large stores but if she has to pay she writes out a cheque from her account at bankers Coutts & Co.

Usually her detective stays by her car, which is invariably parked illegally on a double yellow line. His job is to stop anyone tampering with the car, but primarily he keeps away hovering traffic wardens and wheel-clamp teams. Prince Charles has ticked her off for accumulating so many parking tickets and pictures in the papers showing her car illegally parked. 'You must set a better example,' he told her irritably.

While Princess Diana's enjoyment of shopping is well known, her passion for ballet is not. Like Princess Margaret, she loves watching ballet rehearsals and is often to be found chatting to the dancers of the London City Ballet who practise in fashionable Covent Garden or in a studio underneath the arches behind Kings Cross station. As patron she receives regular newsletters telling her in detail about their activities. She even ticked them off for not giving her enough of the bad news about the troupe.

The Princess always wanted to be a ballet dancer, but at 5 ft 10½ ins grew too tall and had to give up her dream. It was such a burning desire that as a teenager she would often spend hours at her Althorp home in Northamptonshire practising movements to music played on a battered record player.

Diana now lives the life of a dancer vicariously. At least once a week she rolls back the carpet in her sitting room for a ninety minute workout session under the gaze of a female instructor from a reputable ballet school. She warms up with bar work and then practises moves in the centre of the room. 'It's a combination of tap, jazz and ballet and I really enjoy it enormously,' she says. 'I think it's vital to switch off for one or two hours a week. It's my absolute passion.'

The diminutive Harold King, artistic director of the London City Ballet is delighted she is so keen. 'The routine is very demanding. By the end of it you droop and really work up a sweat. But it is very good for her.'

It was during her regular weekly dance classes that she learned the moves for her sensational appearance on the stage of Covent Garden with ballet star Wayne Sleep. Before the show stopping performance, the Princess had secretly learned the steps at Kensington Palace. Her dance teacher had taken down the instructions – literally step by step – from Wayne, so that Diana could practise her routine to one of her pop favourites, Billy Joel's 'Uptown Girl'.

Diana's exercise regime is not confined to ballet and swimming. In the summer she plays the occasional game of tennis at the exclusive Queen's Club where the Duchess of Gloucester, Princess Michael and the Duchess of York are members. However for a good half of her life at Kensington Palace she has either been pregnant or recovering from childbirth, and for several summers contented herself with sunbathing in the garden where she picked the rose petals to make sweet-scented pot-pourri. Her father, Lord Spencer, was a regular visitor for afternoon tea, sweeping up the drive in his Rolls Royce to see his two daughters. Traditionally the royal family like to take tea at four o'clock and the Princess is no exception. A tea trolley laden with a selection of sandwiches and homemade fancy cakes is wheeled into her sitting room by her butler.

Like Charles, the Princess enjoys meeting people in the news. Twice she insisted that the Conservative minister's wife, Margaret Tebbit, who was crippled in the Brighton bomb outrage, should come for tea. In the end she agreed and arrived with her husband Norman to meet the Princess and her children. Afterwards Diana showed the wheelchair-bound Mrs Tebbit around their walled garden.

William and Harry are usually the stars of the show, helping to break the social ice; the barriers between the various royal houses come tumbling down with the children. Lady Rose and Lady Davina, the two Gloucester girls, and Laura and Alexandra Fellowes, sister Jane's children, often play with William and Harry in the afternoon. Princess Michael claims that her daughter, Lady Ella, joins in the fun and games too. For a time their favourite 'uncle' was the Prince's former butler, Allan Fisher. He loved chatting to the children and would always give them carnations or roses from the garden to take home to show their parents.

It is a reflection of the new life and vibrancy of Kensington Palace that so many royal children live here. There are so many that at one stage Diana considered setting up a royal kindergarten within the palace. Not for generations have so many royal children enjoyed the delights of watching the nesting mallards in the Serpentine, sailing their sailboats on the Round Pond, or going for promenades in the park with their nannies. The arrival of this new generation of royal children has brought increased attention from photographers – and angered Princess Diana, who is genuinely protective of her children.

One of the few times the world has seen the Spencer steel was when cameramen gathered at the entrance to Kensington Palace to try and photograph young 'Wombat', Charles's affectionate nickname for William. She stopped the car, wound down the window and shouted 'Leave him alone. Alone do you hear. How would you like your children to be treated like that?'

Now that he is at school, the slow dawning of his future role is beginning to break upon William. Diana is trying to shield him from the realization of his fate for as long as possible. She tells friends: 'I want to protect him for as long as possible. When he sees photographers taking pictures, he always asks "Why are they taking pictures of me, mummy?" I tell him that it is not him they have come to see but me. I know it sounds arrogant but so far it has worked.'

Charles too likes to introduce the children gently into their royal roles. When the Red Devils parachute team dropped into Kensington Palace he realized it was an ideal opportunity for his son to review the troops as well. As William wandered down the line of stiff backed soldiers, his hands in his pockets, there were echoes of the day two hundred years ago when Queen Anne's son, the Duke of Gloucester paraded an army of little boys in the same paddock. Young Gloucester, then four, told King William: 'My dear King, you shall have both my companies with you in Flanders.'

Prince Charles puts enormous emphasis on politeness for his children. He says: 'At the end of it, if they are not very bright, or very qualified, at least if they have reasonable manners they will get so much further in life than by not having them.' For all that William is a boisterous boy and has to be watched constantly when he is around the palace. All the panic buttons which are linked to the nearby police lodge had to be moved because William kept pressing them. When he broke a porcelain miniature of Queen Victoria, all the pottery and ornaments were moved out of his reach, and the boys were banned from the drawing room. Besides flushing his father's and his own shoes down the loo, Prince William is notorious for staging great escapes from the palace.

On one occasion William ran out of the front door and into the gravel courtyard while Prince Michael's chauffeur, John Jenkins, was reversing his Jaguar. William was standing in a blind spot and was out of Jenkins's line of vision. Suddenly he saw a movement and braked. At that moment Diana marched out of the house, scooped up her son, and took him back inside. All she saw was a stationary car and an errant son. She never realized the danger to the future king.

Cars fascinate Prince William, much to his nanny's annoyance. He can often be found at the Kensington Palace garages watching the chauffeurs hose down the royal limousines. He jumps in and out of the jets of water and often ends up soaking wet. 'He is a wild one,' observed one staff member. One chase ended up with him falling on some flagstones. 'That will serve you right,' the deputy nanny, Olga Powell told him firmly.

At Highgrove Diana stopped him using a superb miniature Jaguar car that motor apprentices had made him, because he was such a menace. He drove around the estate using the car like a dodgem as he bashed into everything in sight. Now he uses up his energy on his sporty BMX bike, complete with stabilizers, which his parents gave him. The Prince is very proud of his presents and loves to show his toys to visitors. When Jimmy James, the royal shoemaker, comes to fit the boys for shoes, William and Harry immediately drag him up to the nursery. 'They are literally jumping up and down with excitement,' he says.

Prince William's wilful and independent nature can sometimes wound his parents. When Diana returned home from her tour of Japan and Canada she found William's attitude heartbreaking. She told a friend: 'William bounced downstairs, asked for his present and disappeared again.' In fact royal tours are a genuine wrench for Diana. On one tour she was making her nightly call home to the nanny when William came on the line. 'When are you coming up, Mummy?' he asked plaintively. He thought that she was downstairs, preparing for her evening visit to the nursery.

The one place where the boys are likely to be quiet is in Diana's sitting room. She likes to play or watch television with them there after she has arrived home from a day's engagements. The long-running children's television programme, *Blue Peter* is a favourite and William adores the entertainer Rod Hull and Emu. He was so obsessed about them that the Princess invited Rod Hull and his aggressive bird along for a royal children's tea party.

Naturally the Princess reads to her children, makes jigsaws and models and does all the million and one activities every mother enjoys with her children. Most important, it is she and Prince Charles, not their nanny, who are in charge of discipline. It is a sensible royal tradition that only the parents are responsible for physically punishing their children. Nanny's come and go, parents are for life. This rule is observed for all the children living at Kensington Palace.

The Prince and Princess also like to be fully involved at bathtime and in reading a bedtime story. At half-past seven when the children are in bed the royal couple spend their first few minutes of the day together. If time allows they will have supper together in the dining room and catch up on the day's news. Charles then retires to his study where he catches up with his paperwork while listening to Italian opera, with the doors closed and the volume up. In his study he goes through a vigorous routine for fifteen minutes, doing Canadian Air Force training exercises to keep in shape. Even Prince William has been brought up in the keepfit routine. In the school holidays he travels to Knightsbridge every week for fortyfive minutes gymnastics under the watchful eye of former Marine Edward Sturges.

For Prince Charles the activity increases as the skiing season approaches, when he tones up with extra press-ups and knee bends. The rhythmic thud, thud, thud on the ceiling tells everyone he is in training, although there have been many times when he has been found by his butler lying in a mess of paperwork on his desk, sound asleep. Then he is helped to bed in the dressing room so he will not disturb Diana.

If the Princess has nothing planned she will dine alone in her sitting room from a silver tray. She has been known to send out for a takeaway at a local Chinese restaurant. She enjoys crochet and embroiders cushions and samplers while watching soap operas on television. If she has an early night – nine o'clock is not uncommon – she retires with a light romantic novel by her step-grandmother, Barbara Cartland, or Danielle Steele.

However these days the Princess is not entirely content to be the dutiful, stay-at-home wife. She is now a real night owl, happy to leave Prince Charles at home or at an all male dinner – 'his boys' nights' she calls them. There are few West End shows and films she has not seen at least once. 'I always try and see everything,' she says. The long-running *Phantom of the Opera* has been graced by her presence three times (she has dined out with the show's star, Michael Crawford) and she has seen the film *Amadeus* twice and goes with friends such as Catherine Soames to see other shows. Her efforts to embrace an ordinary lifestyle do have their drawbacks however. When she went to see a performance of the sell-out show *Les Miserables* there was not a ticket to be had. Finally she sent an aide to haggle with the ticket touts outside the Cambridge Circus venue to ensure a seat.

On another occasion she was crawling through West End traffic when the traffic lights changed. Her Scotland Yard bodyguards, who follow on her tail in their own car, had to jump the lights and consequently blocked the rest of the traffic. An irate taxi driver told the detective his fortune in no uncertain terms, not realizing that the Princess could hear his four-letter language. When the Princess arrived at the theatre where she was seeing the comedian Rowan Atkinson in his one-man show, she told the police driver with a smile 'I think I understand what the taxi driver was getting at.'

Princess Diana's solo visit to a nightclub during a skiing trip to Switzerland was merely an indication of the other side of Diana's life. In London she regularly visits Italian restaurants on the trendy Kings Road and then occasionally goes to the exclusive, members-only nightclubs. However, more often than not the dining room in Apartments 8 and 9 is buzzing with the sound of lively chatter as the Prince and Princess host a mid-week dinner party. When they were first married they entertained little – in fact their extrovert butler, Allan Fisher, resigned because he found Kensington Palace life too 'boring'. Should he return he would be surprised at the difference. Gone are the days when Diana used to drink Pimms No 1 because she thought it was non-alcoholic. She is now an assured and accomplished society hostess, although she does worry sometimes about where to place the more attractive lady guests. Once when she was ruminating about where to seat a particular lady her butler supplied the answer. 'Ma'am, you could put her on the Prince's lap and it wouldn't matter. At the end of the dinner, she will go out of the door and you will still be here.' Following his advice, the Princess placed the lady next to Prince Charles.

The couple's Kensington Palace dinner parties are roughly divided into those for friends and family, those for the world of politics, art and showbusiness, and those where Prince Charles holds court, inviting leading members of various professions to meet and discuss their specialization. All are reasonably formal, black tie and long dress affairs. The ladies follow tradition by leaving after dinner to allow the men to carry on their discussions over port. Cheese is never served, nor do the royal couple use fish knives and forks when they serve fish. 'So middle class.' Prince Charles is a notoriously slow eater and is often the last to finish a course. If he ever feels a guest needs to be put at ease he has a simple psychological technique to relax them. Shortly after the meal has started he will say: 'Pass the bloody salt and pepper, will you?' There is no need for use of the swear word, it is his coded way of saying that he is in fact quite human and that the discussion can be frank and free.

During these black tie affairs the atmosphere is relaxed. Diana will often bring the children in to say goodnight. Indeed when William and Harry were babies she loved nothing more than to show the infants off to her friends.

While the Prince and Princess of Wales entertain frequently, invitations to other royal residents inside Kensington Palace are rare. Only the Gloucesters and Princess Margaret have been for dinner although once when Diana was pregnant with Prince Harry she did invite Princess Michael for lunch. Charles likes to use the Duke of Gloucester as a sounding board for his ideas on architecture (Prince Richard is a trained architect), while Diana and Princess Margaret have a common interest in the ballet.

When dinner is over Prince Charles, ever the gentleman, will walk Princess Margaret the few yards to her front door. However they don't go outside; they use a secret network of underground passageways which crisscross the palace. In the event of a nuclear attack these catacombs (they are on two floors) would be used as fallout shelters by the royals and their members of staff.

Of the other members of the royal family, Prince Andrew is a regular visitor, even wandering in and out of Diana's dressing room while she is having her hair cut. They have been friends since childhood, and as a teenager Diana used to joke with her school friends that one day she would like to marry the Prince. She caught the bigger fish, but during Prince Andrew's romance with Sarah Ferguson Diana was the go-between, passing on messages, providing encouragement and letting them use Kensington Palace as a safe haven. Diana even steered Andrew to take the plunge when he began to get cold feet.

Prince Edward is an occasional visitor (although he is closer to Princess Anne) but it is the Queen and Prince Philip who have rarely if ever been guests at the Prince and Princess's home. The relationship between the Queen and Princess Diana is strictly one between a mother-in-law and a new wife, cordial but distant, in sharp contrast to the warm chatty friendship the Duchess of York has quickly built up with the Chairman of the Family Firm. From the start Diana was determined to go her own way, a headstrong move implicitly condoned by her father Earl Spencer. He says: 'I know the royals can seem to swallow people up when they marry in. But that would never happen to us. We've been brought up with royalty and there is no question of us being pushed out.'

When Diana entered the royal family she came with the awareness that her family were as English as the oak. By comparison the Mountbatten-Windsors were Johnny-come-latelys.

The coolness between the Princess and the Queen was characterized by an incident at Balmoral. When the Queen was returning from a picnic in a Land Rover with a group of friends, she happened to pass the Princess taking Harry for a walk. As they drove by in a cloud of dust the Queen remarked, somewhat sorrowfully 'I never get an invitation to see them, you know. It is so difficult seeing the boys.'

While the Queen has been frozen out, a large number of European and Middle Eastern royalty do enjoy the royal couple's hospitality. King Hussein of Jordan and his American born wife Queen Noor are regular guests, as is his brother, Crown Prince Hassan. Ex-King Constantine of Greece, together with leading English aristocrats, such as the Duke and Duchess of Westminster and Lord and Lady Romsey, are often invited.

While the Prime Minister, Mrs Thatcher, and her husband Denis have been to dinner at Kensington Palace, Prince Charles is closer to the former Labour Prime Minister James Callaghan and the former Speaker of the House of Commons, Lord Tonypandy. The couple also entertain other leading politicians such as Dr David Owen and Labour leader Neil Kinnock, as well as friends from the world of commerce such as Lord King, the chairman of British Airways. Invitations to dinner often have a purpose. The film maker Sir Richard Attenborough went along to give Diana a few tips on how to behave in front of the cameras for her famous interview with Sir Alastair Burnet. Television veteran Jimmy Savile suggested that the Princess might like to involve herself in the 'Say No' anti-drugs campaign. To his delight she agreed and has gone on to take a leading role in the campaign.

The royal couple have hosted a series of dinners for Fleet Street editors in the hope of gaining more privacy. The soft sell worked; most of these hard-bitten characters came away walking on air. 'Her eyes, I could die for her eyes,' said one.

Occasionally the royal couple will literally ask their guests to sing for their supper. Opera stars Placido Domingo, Luciano Pavarotti, Sir Geraint Evans and Kiri Te Kanawa have all given private performances for Charles, Diana and their guests. For schoolboy soprano Aled Jones it was the highlight of his career to be asked to sing for them.

While these are glittering social gatherings the Prince has also made Kensington Palace an informal intellectual club where academics from different spheres can exchange ideas and ideals. In his own way Prince Charles has taken to heart the dictum of Victorian constitutionalist Walter Bagehot, that the monarch's prerogatives are to 'be consulted, to encourage and to warn'. He sees these guidelines as applicable also to his nebulous and undefined role as the Prince of Wales.

The Prince consults a wide range of political and social groupings, encourages charities and organizations by taking an active interest in their work and issues warnings as he sees fit in his various speeches and in his private conversations with government ministers, overseas diplomats and politicians. Kensington Palace is the hub of this work, the centre for a number of serious dinners and lunches where the Prince's concerns for the disabled, alternative (or, as the Prince prefers to call it, complementary) medicine, architecture, conservation, organic farming and race relations are on the agenda. The Prince has said: 'I give lunches and dinners at Kensington Palace and try and encourage a different awareness, approach or attitude towards a problem.'

At one dinner held at Kensington Palace, Prince Charles and Sir Laurens van der Post sat talking well into the night to a world famous nuclear scientist. Physics and psychology came together and the sparks flew.

By sheer contrast, on the night that Prince Charles brought the leading physicians from London hospitals together to discuss the value of complementary medicine with its practitioners, Princess Michael was hosting a glitzy showbusiness dinner next door for people such as Selina Scott and David Frost.

It was a seminar at Kensington Palace that altered the Prince's whole approach to farming. The meeting, involving farmers, scientists and conservationists, discussed alternative farming methods. Organic farmer Lawrence Woodward and conservationist Dr Miriam Rothschild were present. The quality of argument was such that the Prince agreed to visit an organic project near Newbury, Berkshire. The result was that he bought the 420-acre Broadfield Farm to add to the 350 acres he owned at Highgrove. Much of this is now being organically farmed and the animals treated with homoeopathic medicine when possible.

From evening seminars and morning meetings, to Knightsbridge shopping trips and lunchtime gossips, the Prince and Princess of Wales have their private routine at Kensington Palace. For their Kensington Palace staff there is a separate rhythm that must fit in completely with the Prince and Princess's lives. For instance, every Friday afternoon at one, as regular as clockwork, grey haired Mr Pusey walks up the drive to wind up every clock in Kensington Palace. He times his weekly visits to perfection, tiptoeing into the drawing and dining rooms with his array of winding instruments when he knows that the royal couple will be out.

Every Wednesday a black and gold liveried van from Sycamore Laundry arrives outside the back door of Apartments 8 and 9 to pick up a sturdy wicker basket containing the week's dirty washing. Every piece is dutifully noted and logged in a special black book. It is returned neatly folded and interleaved with tissue paper. John the milkman brings several crates of milk every morning at half-past nine. Only Clarence House and Buckingham Palace get crested milk from the Royal Dairy at Windsor Castle – at Kensington Palace they have to make do with Unigate. However, three days a week the Royal Dairy delivers their own make of cream cheese. The Kensington Palace meat comes from a wholesale butcher in Smithfield market who delivers only to the royal family; their fish is brought fresh daily by an Essex fishmonger. These activities go unnoticed, shading into the background of palace life, just like the Department of the Environment workers who pick up the rubbish from carved wooden boxes outside each apartment twice daily, and keep the palace tidy.

In the grounds surrounding the royal apartments the servicing and maintenance is carried out unobtrusively, while inside the apartments the royal staff know instinctively that their job is to be seen when needed and never heard. The bell governs their lives, indicating that Upstairs wants service from Downstairs. 'I even hear the bloody bell when I'm on holiday,' one member of staff moaned.

Apartments 8 and 9 have the largest number of employees by far. The Prince and Princess recruited their staff in the tried and tested manner; from the Forces, from employment agencies and by word of mouth. Prince Charles, for example, 'poached' his chef Mervyn Wycherley from the Queen's kitchens at Buckingham Palace. Their employees are divided into three distinct groups, Household, Officials and Staff. The Household are the equivalent of senior executives, the Officials of white collar workers, the Staff of blue collar workers.

At Kensington Palace Prince Charles and his family normally have sixteen staff to look after them. Their butler, two valets for Prince Charles, two dressers for the Princess, two nannys (one part-time) two cooks, two chauffeurs, an orderly, a housekeeper, and three fulltime cleaners. In addition there are the Scotland Yard bodyguards who are never more than a pace behind their royal charges. At least one sleeps in the staff quarters every night.

Since the royal couple have moved into Kensington Palace they have suffered a rapid turnover of employees; most notably there has been the departure of Prince Charles's private secretary, Edward Adeane, his valet Stephen Barry, and the nanny Barbara Barnes. The exodus of staff produced the telling phrase 'malice at the palace' to describe the poisonous atmosphere inside Apartments 8 and 9. Diana was blamed as the hard-hearted culprit, Charles the other-wordly wimp who bowed to his wife's demands. As one royal wag put it: 'When Diana was at school she won the prize for the best kept guinea pig, now she has got the best kept mouse.' These stories, which were good for gossip, merely added another veneer of confusion to the picture of the royal couple's home life.   -

The reality is more complex. To begin with a number of household staff only have short term contracts. These are the diplomats and the military officers seconded for three-year periods as assistant private secretaries, equerries and administrators. Other fulltime staff such as cleaners and chauffeurs have only marginal contact with the royal family and receive their orders from others. Many staff leave because of the poor pay – even butler Harold Brown does outside catering work to bolster his meagre pay packet – others because once the initial glamour of working for the most famous couple in the world has worn off they find the life unexciting.

Then there are the personality clashes both upstairs and downstairs that occur in any company, particularly one run on a servant–master principle. Charles's accountant Michael Colbourne, a former grammar school boy, was driven out by the snobbery of Household staff. He was an Official rather than a member of the Household and because he did not wear the old public school tie found that his face did not fit. The ultimate insult occurred when he was excluded from the annual staff party with the Prince and Princess because he was not 'one of us'. Equally, the downstairs staff were not amused the day they were lined up for a pep talk by the new Comptroller of the Household, Lieutenant-Colonel Philip Creasey. 'We all have to make economies now,' he told them. The cut-backs started with the Prince and Princess of Wales turning off lights wherever they went, a trait common to many millionaire home owners.

These explanations aside, it is true to say that the atmosphere, certainly in the early days, was unhappy. Both the Prince and the Princess were finding their way in new roles, and the staff suffered accordingly. In a way, the royal couple suffered from the Princess Margaret syndrome. When she first married and moved into Kensington Palace a number of her staff left within the first few months. Now she has the most contented and loyal staff of any member of the royal family. Similarly, when Prince Charles and Princess Diana moved to Kensington Palace there was a haemmorrhage of resignations, forced or otherwise, which has now been staunched to a trickle.

Much of the problem stems from Prince Charles's own personality. He is a man who likes staff around him who are characters, people who don't forever bow and scrape and who will, if necessary, tell him what to do; people who will amuse him, argue with him, yet ultimately who defer to his will, if that is what he wishes. In his bachelor days he was surrounded by an unusual combination of exceptional, larger-than-life characters. His valet Stephen Barry, a notorious homosexual who later died of AIDS, pampered the Prince and ironed out all his household problems. He enjoyed a highly privileged position. No valet before or since has ever accompanied the Prince of Wales on a walkabout. The ever-dapper Barry did, smartly walking a couple of paces behind his master, basking in the royal limelight.

Naturally his presence infuriated the new Princess of Wales, who saw him as in some way usurping her role. The crunch came when he walked into their master bedroom one morning while Diana was in her grey silk nightie. With a coldly polite 'Good morning, Your Royal Highness' he proceeded to walk around the bedroom opening the curtains, folding back the sheets, plumping the pillows – and totally ignoring the presence of the Princess. That was the final straw. As one of Barry's closest colleagues told me: 'There was only room for one Princess of Wales – and Diana was determined it was going to be her.'

Diana's brother, Viscount Althorp, was rather more euphemistic: 'In a quiet way she has weeded out a lot of the hangers-on who surrounded Charles.' Barry was certainly one, but other members of staff had decided to make a move from royal service once the Prince got married. His bodyguard, Chief Inspector Paul Officer, and Superintendent John Maclean were typical. Paul Officer, who once saved Charles's life when the Prince was attacked by a demented fellow-officer when he was in the Navy, had a powerful intellectual influence. It is not generally realized that royal bodyguards spend more time with the royal family than anyone else. Often a close bond of friendship – and power – builds up. Prince Edward calls one detective who has been with him since childhood days 'Dad'. On long car journeys Charles and Chief Inspector Officer would chat for hours about everything from mysticism and runes, to the after life and vegetarianism. His bodyguard was fascinated by these esoteric subjects and even lent the Prince books by the Swedish Christian and former secretary-general of the UN Dag Hammarsjöld. Certainly Officer, a strict vegetarian, helped convince the Prince to strike meat off his diet. But Charles's first attempt to put principle into practise did not go down well with the rest of the royal family. It was over dinner at Balmoral that Charles first made his feelings known. 'I've given up eating meat,' he told the Queen as he was offered a piece of venison. The Queen gave him one of those famous looks that freeze over the Sahara: 'Grow up,' she snapped, and continued with her dinner. Charles took his piece of meat.

Besides Officer and Barry, the Boss, as Charles was called, was served by Chief Superintendent John Maclean, a tough Glaswegian so untidy he makes Bob Geldof seem like a shop window mannequin. John, whose motto was 'I will kill for them but I won't die for them', was the rough equivalent of Charles's court jester. 'My cultural advisor,' was Charles's ironic description of this colourful character. He took the notion of '*lèse majesté*' to its limits, waving to people from the car when Charles was asleep. On one occasion he was with the Prince when he was shooting wild boar in Liechtenstein with Crown Prince Hans and his German cousins. After the day's sport the two Princes approached Maclean. Charles said 'We've done well today.' Maclean, who is indifferent to blood sports, said flatly 'You would be better off gassing them.' Even Charles was taken aback.

Yet John was an excellent policeman and a superb skier, and was sadly missed when he chose to take early retirement. The idea of him being tyrannised by Diana into leaving is laughable. However she did have a hand in the removal of her one-time private secretary, Oliver Everett, the man who cradled Charles in his arms after he collapsed during a polo match in Palm Beach, Florida. 'Won't you get rid of this bloody man,' she reportedly said to Charles in front of him. He left to become the Queen's librarian at Windsor, and his departure was matched by a flow of departures of downstairs staff. Their butler Allan Fisher, together with dressers, cooks, chauffeurs, and cleaners all went elsewhere. Certainly in the early days the atmosphere in the apartment was poisonous. The couple would row so frequently that a senior Buckingham Palace courtier was moved to tell visitors 'Don't worry if they argue in front of you, just ignore it. Their rows don't last long.' The most flagrant example was the night that the royal couple were scheduled to join the Queen and the rest of the family at the Royal Albert Hall for the Festival of Remembrance. Diana, straining to lose weight after the birth of Prince William, told Charles that she didn't feel like going and asked him to stay at Kensington Palace as well. A ferocious argument developed which ended with her in tears and Charles insisting that he had to attend the service. In a haunting phrase that could sum up any royal marriage he told her: 'My duty lies above my loyalty to you.' Then he stalked out. Several minutes later she had a change of heart. In spite of her puffy eyes and streaked makeup she decided to go. A member of staff, who has since left, remembers pleading with the Princess to stay at home and fake an excuse. 'There is nothing worse you can do than arrive after the Queen,' he argued. She ignored him and turned up at the Royal Albert Hall five minutes after the royal party had sat down. Even her chair had been removed from the royal box, and when she appeared an official hastily had to recover it. Still the couple's row continued in the darkness of the royal box. It was so heated that Prince Philip, embarrassed, moved his chair so that he could screen the warring couple from the audience.

Behind the door at Kensington Palace staff frequently saw the royal mask slipping. Diana would sit sobbing in her bedroom, saying time and again 'I'm a failure, I'm a failure'. She resented the fact that she was blamed for the departure of every staff member. Her simmering anger surfaced during one royal visit when she rounded on her Press Boswell, the corpulent James Whitaker of the *Daily Mirror*, and snapped 'I want you to understand that I am not responsible for any sackings. I don't just sack people.' That outburst came during the most disturbing and enigmatic resignation, that of Prince Charles's private secretary Edward Adeane.

Adeane, a libel lawyer who was expected to guide Charles to the throne, left abruptly and did not even wait until a replacement was found. Again, the answer lies more with the Prince than the Princess, although he found her indifferent to his counsel. 'If I ever see another knitted bootee I'll go mad,' Adeane reportedly said. However as the Prince became more under the sway of outside advisors such as Sir Laurens van der Post and Dr Armand Hammer, Adeane felt that his role was being undercut, his schedules rewritten, his advice overruled.

While hostile towards some former staff, Princess Diana is remarkable chummy with others. It is significant that those closest to her when she married – her dresser Evelyn Dagley, her lady-in-waiting Anne Beckwith-Smith, and her two bodyguards Inspector Graham Smith and Sergeant Alan Peters – have all stayed with her. She calls them by their first names, remembers their birthdays and has even dropped in for tea with the wife of bodyguard Graham Smith at his north London home.

The one major departure from Diana's side has been her nanny Barbara Barnes. Miss Barnes, daughter of a Norfolk farm worker, had intended to stay with the young family until Prince William was at least ten years old. She came from Lady Glenconner, a lady-in-waiting to Princess Margaret, with impeccable references and immediately impressed the royal couple with her unfussy, no nonsense style. While she struck up a friendly relationship with Princess Diana – 'She never said a hard word about Diana,' says a friend – she never found Prince Charles as easy going. He has rather more than a fatherly interest in the upbringing of his boys, particularly William. It is unlikely that Charles will become King until he is a pensioner and so, like Edward VII who followed Queen Victoria, he will reign for a relatively short time. It is William who will face the burden of carrying the British monarchy into the twenty-first century. For that reason every aspect of his development has concerned Charles. Yet Nanny Barnes found his incessant meddling hard to take. She had considered resigning when William was just a toddler. However, a late night pep talk with Superintendent John Maclean convinced her to stay.

It was said in royal circles that Prince Charles longed for a nanny more in the mould of the starchy and strict Mabel Anderson, who reared all the Queen's children. 'A child wouldn't dare pick up his knife and fork without Mabel Anderson saying so,' says a fellow royal nanny admiringly. Nanny Barnes had a more liberal regime and it seems that Prince Charles was not happy with the way William was turning out. Perhaps his boisterous behaviour in Westminster Abbey when he was pageboy to the Duke and Duchess of York was a turning point. It certainly provoked considerable comment of the 'king of the brat pack' variety. When Miss Barnes left in January 1987, the day William went to his prep school, Princess Diana went out of her way to tell pensioners at an old peoples' home just how polite and well-mannered William was. A coincidence – or her subtle way of letting the world know that as far as she was concerned there was nothing wrong with her eldest son?

Diana quickly found a replacement, a former nurse and social worker who had been the part-time nanny to Princess Michael's children. But Nanny Ruth Wallace's departure did not please Princess Michael, who was one of the last to know. Like other royals, Princess Michael guards her staff jealously and does not like to see them being poached by rival households.

The atmosphere within Apartments 8 and 9 is now calmer, the tempo more even. There are fewer explosions, fewer surprises, fewer tears and tantrums. Within their marriage the royal couple have developed their separate lives. Their staff have settled to their task. The downstairs myths about malice at the palace mirror the upstairs legends surrounding the royal couple. The truth lies disguised within this kaleidoscope of contrasting images. Yet the fierce light that beats upon a royal marriage, to paraphrase Tennyson, has never shone so brightly as upon the life of Prince Charles and Princess Diana; although it is a light that has often blinded rather than enlightened. In the dappled shade of Kensington Palace Diana and Charles find peace, sanctuary and a chance to lead a secret personal life.

As the red helicopter heads for the distant horizon after unloading its royal cargo, the front door of the royal apartment closes tightly. As the rest of the world is shut out the real Diana opens up – the Princess behind closed doors.

4

The Royal Outsiders
The Prince and Princess *Michael of Kent*

Lord Mountbatten fixed the newly-married Princess Michael of Kent with a baleful stare. His advice was short, sharp and to the point. 'Madam,' he said sternly, 'the best thing you can do is keep your mouth shut.'

His words of warning, spoken during an intimate dinner party at the Michael's London home – Apartment 10, Kensington Palace – went unheeded. Princess Michael, blonde, statuesque, imperious, has gone her own wilful way since she married Prince Michael in 1978. 'I may be many things but I am not boring,' the Princess is proud of boasting.

She has been the shooting star in the royal firmament, exuding an incandescent charm, yet wayward and unpredicatable. Lord Mountbatten realized the problems after he took up her cause when she and Prince Michael wished to marry. Born Marie-Christine von Riebnitz, the potential Princess was a divorced Catholic descended from minor European aristocracy. Mountbatten undertook the tricky diplomatic task of convincing the Queen that Marie-Christine was a suitable candidate for the hand of her cousin. According to his former private secretary, John Barratt, he warned the Queen that if she did not give way Prince Michael would live with the Czech born beauty and cause a greater scandal. A measure of Mountbatten's skill was that the Queen granted the newly-weds a grace-and-favour home at Kensington Palace.

Their ten room house – the smallest royal apartment – was dubbed 'the dolls house' by Princess Margaret when she and Anthony Armstrong-Jones moved there for the first years of their ill-fated marriage. For Prince Michael the palace was familiar territory. He and his brother, the Duke of Kent, and sister, Princess Alexandra, had been brought up there by their mother, the elegant Princess Marina. When his brother and sister married, Prince Michael had used his mother's apartment as a London base.

Within the royal family he was a popular young bachelor, only making the headlines with his daredevil exploits on the bob sleigh runs of St Moritz or on gruelling car rallies. Mild mannered and affable, Princess Marina's youngest child seemed destined for a role in the royal chorus until Marie-Christine came along.

While Prince Michael's arrival at Kensington Palace was welcomed by its royal residents, the hand of friendship did not extend to the new Princess. Her character had already marked her out for adverse critical comment. The Princess, glamorous, glossy and chic, did not conform to the established British way of behaviour. She was too enthusiastic about her new royal role, wearing her ambition on her sleeve rather than in her back pocket.

Within the royal family, feelings ran much deeper. The Duke and Duchess of Gloucester could not forgive and forget that Marie-Christine's affair with Prince Michael started during a country weekend party at their Northamptonshire home, Barnwell Manor. At the time she was married to their close friend, merchant banker Tom Troubridge, and they had watched with growing anger the clandestine relationship between Marie-Christine and Prince Michael.

It is a measure of their friendship that Troubridge is still a regular dinner guest at the Gloucesters' home. They remembered too that before her marriage to Tom Troubridge, she had romanced the Duke's elder brother, Prince William, who was tragically killed in an aircraft crash. Senior staff at Kensington Palace believe that Prince William, who was in line to become the Duke of Gloucester, was so smitten by Marie-Christine that he asked the Queen to give her consent for permission to marry her. The Queen is said to have refused this request. Whether or not she was formally asked can never finally be proved. What is the case is that the story is widely believed within Kensington Palace.

However the Gloucesters are not alone in their disapproval. Princess Margaret, a staunch and deeply religious Anglican, disliked the Princess's Catholicism and was resentful of the fact that Marie-Christine was a divorcee who had been allowed to marry into the royal family, whereas a generation before Princess Margaret had been prevented in her wish to marry the divorced equerry, Group Captain Peter Townsend.

Lady Colin Campbell summed up Princess Margaret's attitude in one pithy sentence. 'Princess Margaret would rather drink a cup of poison than have a drink with Princess Michael.' When Princess Margaret spotted Marie-Christine at a West End restaurant she totally ignored her. 'I would not put them together round my dinner table,' says one socialite who knows them both well. The hostility was reflected by Princess Margaret's son, Viscount Linley; in an interview with *Ritz* magazine he was asked what he would give his worst enemy for Christmas. His ascerbic reply: 'Dinner with Princess Michael of Kent' created widespread support for Princess Michael, although within the royal family the *bon mot* was rather enjoyed. The remark had wider repercussions within Kensington Palace. Princess Michael was furious about it and wrote a stinging memo of complaint to Princess Margaret.

Princess Michael told her friends: 'I have always made allowances for that boy [referring to the divorce between Lord Snowdon and Princess Margaret] but I didn't even get an apology.' Ironically, honour was settled when Prince Michael tackled Linley face to face as they went to dinner at the family Christmas party at Windsor. The bearded Prince Michael, who has a tough streak that belies his meek image, was at his combative best. 'What was the meaning of that remark?' he asked Linley angrily. Without waiting for a reply he went on: 'Explain yourself. I hope you realize that you are talking about the woman who is my wife, the woman I love and the woman that *you* don't know.' For once Linley was totally tongue-tied and slunk away from this royal battle of wills. But his ordeal was not over. Princess Michael collared him later and hissed: 'Don't ever speak to me again, you disgusting boy.'

Again it was at Christmas, the time of goodwill towards men, that Princess Margaret made her feelings known about her neighbour. She was hosting a seasonal party for her staff and friends from other royal houses. She went around the room chatting amiably to one and all. Then she paused and began to shake hands with an unknown Kensington Palace worker. 'He is employed by Princess Michael of Kent,' explained a servant helpfully. Margaret's face creased in horror. She quickly withdrew her hand and moved on to the next group without a word. One surprised guest remarked: 'I have never seen anything like that in my life.'

As far as Princess Margaret is concerned her own staff can do no wrong – even when they upset Princess Michael. On one occasion Princess Michael complained about the rusty hulk of an American car owned by the son of Princess Margaret's chef, Stanislaw Wasneiski. She felt that the gaudy red vehicle was an eyesore and wrote to the police about it. In turn they approached Stan and asked him to tow it away.

Viscount Linley happened to be passing and took Stan's side. 'You don't have to do that,' he argued. 'You've got permission. See my mum about it.' Stan, who didn't want to cause a fuss, demurred. But Linley insisted and marched off to see his mother, muttering a colourful description of Princess Michael under his breath. Princess Margaret was told of the contretemps and came down to the kitchen especially to see Stan. 'Chef,' she told him, 'you have my permission to leave the car where it is. I am going to ask Lord Napier [her private secretary] to write to Princess Michael about it.' The car stayed where it was until finally it went to the breaker's yard.

Princess Michael has had no further luck in her relations with her direct next-door neighbour, Prince Charles. She once moaned to Mountbatten that Charles had written to her complaining that her 'grand behaviour' was bringing the royal family into disrepute. He made his feelings towards 'MC' – the royal family's nickname for Marie-Christine – perfectly clear at Royal Ascot one year. He whispered to his girlfriend at the time, Anna Wallace, not to curtsey to the Princess.

Ironically, for a time Princess Michael held Charles in high esteem, admiring his 'moral qualities'. Yet even though she was his next-door neighbour, the Princess was both in awe of him and reluctant to approach him directly. When the Pope visited England in 1982, the Catholic Princess was desperate for an audience. She knew that Charles was due to meet him at Canterbury Cathedral and longed to take part herself. For once her nerve failed her. She was afraid to ask the Prince directly to smooth the path for an audience with His Holiness. Rather pathetically she was reduced to pleading with a servant who had once worked for Prince Charles to intercede on her behalf. 'Please can you do anything to help me,' she asked. The staff member, not wishing to get involved in matters above his station, politely declined.

However any hopes that Prince Charles would prove an ally were finally crushed when the Red Devils display team dropped in on Kensington Palace. The main sponsor of the charity parachute jump was Robert Maxwell, publisher of the *Daily Mirror*. His proposed visit came just weeks after the *Mirror* had revealed details about the Nazi SS past of Princess Michael's father, Baron Gunther von Riebnitz. She was horrified that Charles could play host to the Czech-born publisher who she felt had a personal vendetta against her. The Princess wrote several long memos to the Prince, pleading her case that the millionaire publisher should be banned from the palace. Her entreaties fell on deaf ears. The visit went ahead as scheduled, although the Princess made the point of being out when Maxwell arrived.

In public the Princess has continued to put a charitable light on her relationship with Charles. Recalling the day he nearly ran her over as he was entering Kensington Palace in his old Aston Martin she said: 'He'd seen a cripple, and, you know how good he is, he turned round and waved at him as he was turning into the drive.'

The Princess is chummier with Diana, who she calls the 'beautiful Sloane Princess'. Diana took pity on Marie-Christine during her ordeal by media following the revelations about her father's war record. 'Princess Diana was the staunchest friend and I'll never hear a word against her,' she says. Yet that still didn't stop her complaining the day that Prince Harry arrived home. There were so many vans – including a horse-drawn dray – delivering flowers and presents to the Princess's apartment that Princess Michael asked them to unload in the drive because they were making so much noise. It may have been a misunderstanding when she complained to the Royal Protection Squad about the noise a choir was making when they serenaded Diana outside her apartment, on the occasion of her twenty-first birthday.

Away from the immediate royal residents of Kensington Palace, Princess Michael's relations with other members of the royal family are frosty or nonexistent. Prince Michael's brother, the Duke of Kent, is not as close as he might have been, following a bitter row over the couple's Alsatian dog when they spent the weekend at the Kents' country home of Anmer Hall. The disagreement was so vicious that the Michaels returned to London a day earlier than planned. Normally the litmus test of popularity within the royal family is the number of occasions one is invited for lunch with the Queen Mother at Clarence House. Although low in the official royal pecking order, the Michaels have never received an invitation. It is noticeable that Princess Alexandra, technically on a lower rung in the royal hierarchy, visits Clarence House often.

The nadir of Princess Michael's relations with the royal family came during Christmas 1986 when Princess Michael refused to face the rest of the royal clan. She decided against joining the rest of the family for dinner and instead ordered a tray to be sent to her room in the Edward III tower, assigned to her by the Queen. The following morning Princess Michael received a stiff memorandum from the Queen insisting that in future she follow custom and eat with the rest of the royal family. Whether it was by accident or design, during that same Christmas, Princess Michael was the only adult royal to ride in a hired bus with the children from the church service in St George's chapel back to Windsor Castle for lunch on Christmas Day.

While Princess Michael often talks airily about chatting to the Queen about family matters, the truth is that they rarely converse. As any chairman of a large company, the Queen conducts her affairs through memorandums. Private secretary speaks to private secretary, butler to butler, valet to valet. The Queen never rings Princess Michael, nor does she write frequently. One of her most recent letters came during an exchange of memos regarding the merits of riding side-saddle. Princess Michael had wished to learn this tricky technique and had asked the Queen, who used to ride side-saddle for Trooping the Colour, for her advice. The correspondence culminated with a request by the Princess asking if she could stable her horses on the Queen's property at Hampton Court Palace. The Queen raised no objection.

However the Queen has made a summer visit to Princess Michael's home, when she came for tea. Understandably, both Prince and Princess Michael were edgy beforehand. As a thoughtful hostess, Marie-Christine had asked the chefs at Buckingham Palace to prepare the Queen's favourite chocolate cake in advance and had ordered the Queen's own special blend of tea from Harrods. Although it was a bright sunny day the Queen arrived in a fur wrap which Prince Michael quickly took off her shoulders when he and his wife greeted her at the door. The Prince said: 'Hello Lillibet' and then gave her the royal greeting of a kiss on the right cheek, one on the left and a third on the hand, followed by a stiff-necked bow. Princess Michael, who was not nearly so familiar, curtsied deeply and addressed the Queen as 'Ma'am' throughout the forty-five minute visit.

After the usual pleasantries were exchanged, Princess Michael asked gaily: 'Would you like to see the house?' and proceeded to lecture the Queen on her decor. While impressed by the faultless taste of Princess Michael's London home, the Queen only came alive when she went to the nursery to play with Lord Freddie and Lady Ella. Formalities continued with tea in the dining room. Unlike most people, the Queen does not have tea sitting at a low table with a plate perched on her knee. It is an elaborate affair with china teacups, plates and the best silver. Dainty crustless white sandwiches, chocolate Bath Olivers and chocolate cake are the standard fare.

Having exchanged more small talk the Queen left, when the same protocol was observed, Princess Michael curtsying to the floor as the royal car swept out of the courtyard. While the Queen is not noted for her love of interior design, she was suitably surprised by Princess Michael's skill in transforming a dowdy apartment (previously occupied by Sir Philip Haye, director of Sotheby's and formerly Princess Marina's private secretary) into a chic home that exudes a self-assured style.

While their home is the smallest of the royal apartments – in keeping with their status within the family – it is also the nearest to the public footpath that runs alongside the royal apartments. When Princess Margaret lived there she used to sit in the garden and listen to the gossip of visitors to the nearby State Apartments. She called the passing commotion 'my public footsteps'. However the 'public footsteps' of the cleaners of the State Apartments walking to work did not please Princess Michael when she moved in. She objected to their dawn chorus when the women, many of them West Indian, sang gospel tunes as they passed under her bedroom window. Her complaints stilled the early morning anthem. However, inside Princess Michael's home all is peace and quiet, a hymn to elegant good taste.

The Princess used all her abilities to stamp her personality on the apartment. She is proud of her creation and attention to detail. She says: 'There is not a lightswitch in the house that is not designed by me. Rooms are like people, they don't have to be grand or even in great good taste to be fascinating. People have charisma, rooms have atmosphere and that's what counts.' Fellow interior designers are genuinely impressed by her outstanding ability as a decorator. One said admiringly: 'She is very talented, with a wonderful sense of colour and the ability to put a scheme together. The Princess has the unique gift of arranging pieces of furniture and paintings and finding the appropriate textiles for them. She prefers working with wool, cotton and silk and is not afraid of working with expensive or important works of art.' Her friend Ingrid Seward, editor of *Majesty*, is equally complimentary. 'The Princess has decorated her home with flair and imagination. Little things like putting ribbons on the pictures to hide the string show her keen eye.'

The Princess's attention to detail is such that in her kitchen she asked her decorator, Jim Smart, to woodgrain all the units, including the dishwasher, washing machine and tumble drier so that everything matched.

What is also surprising is that Prince Michael is extremely knowledgeable about textiles and about design, yet he made few decisions about the layout of their London home. The interior decorating was entirely the work of his wife, Marie-Christine.

The Princess's pronounced personality does make her the despair of her suppliers. 'Sometimes you just want to throw something at her,' said one. 'She is a difficult client because she knows exactly what she wants and has exacting standards. In fairness that is true of many high-class interior designers.'

The house is on three storeys and everywhere there are reminders of whose home you are visiting. Pictures of Marie-Christine are everywhere, from a large romantic oil painting in the dining room to gilt-framed photographs of her bare shouldered, her thick mane of blonde hair flowing over her shoulders. Her pride and joy is the drawing room, which she spent weeks labouring over to get precisely the way she wanted it. Such is her streak of perfection that woe-betide any cleaner who moves a piece of furniture or *objet d'art*. Everything has its place and position.

Expensive fabrics by the late Spanish designer Fortuny are favoured; Fabergé picture frames, eggs and cigar boxes provide the decoration. The Princess herself designed the glass coffee table, which has an intricate series of velvet lined drawers to house the couple's collection of Fabergé left them by Princess Marina. Other family heirlooms such as the silver Seals of England which belonged to Queen Mary, and fine antique glass with the letter N inscribed on it from Prince Nicholas of Greece, give the room a truly regal feeling. This is underlined by the portraits of Princess Alice, Countess of Athlone, Queen Mary, Prince Michael's father the Duke of Kent, and miniature oils of Charles II's children.

The lighting system, again designed by the Princess, is subtle and unique. Discreet spotlights cast an almost square light on to two Italian Renaissance oil paintings, which hang above a walnut George III chest of drawers.

When the Princess was furnishing her London home she was forever jumping into her Range Rover and driving down to Hampton Court Palace to select pieces from the estate of

Princess Marina. When she died, Marina's collection of fabulous Fabergé eggs, silver plate and furniture was left in the attic at Hampton Court Palace. There was no inventory or any kind of systematic catalogue of this cornucopia of royal memorabilia. As Princess Michael rummaged through the packing cases in the gloom of the attic she would come across priceless Fabergé eggs wrapped in yellowing newspapers, solid silver cutlery strewn in the bottom of cardboard boxes and Prince Michael's childhood toys thrown higgledy-piggledy with valuable glassware and antiques.

The Princess would spend many a happy afternoon cooing over new finds and loading her booty into the back of her car before returning in triumph to Kensington Palace. Tragically, when Hampton Court Palace caught fire, the blaze started directly beneath the attic where the remains of Princess Marina's belongings were stored. Without an inventory, the insurance claim for the remainder of Princess Marina's treasures will have proved difficult.

The Princess spent a lot of time chopping and changing the furniture from Kensington Palace to her country home of Nether Lypiatt in Gloucestershire where the Michaels spend their weekends. For example, a lovely antique table which used to be in the dining room was removed to Nether Lypiatt. In its place Princess Michael bought a cheap table with a hardboard top which is always covered by a tablecloth. The dining room itself is surprisingly small and sparely furnished, dominated by a marble fireplace and an oil painting of the Princess. While the visitor sees many photographs of Marie-Christine and Prince Michael's family, there are no pictures on display of her own family.

It is only in her bedroom that sentiment enters the grand design. In a lighted archway on a wall adjacent to the couple's kingsize bed she displays her small collection of delicate glass swans and photographs of her mother, father and other members of her family. The couple's European ancestry is evident in the Russian religious icons which belonged to Prince Michael's great-grandparents. The legacy of Queen Victoria is shown on the Princess's dressing table where the bracelet and brooch that Prince Albert gave to his beloved wife take pride of place together with a Meissen vase from Princess Marina.

Off the cream carpeted and wallpapered bedroom the couple have a glorious Victorian bathroom en suite, complete with an ancient toilet, pull chain, wood panelling and more pictures of Princess Michael. Across the corridor is their shared study, where Princess Michael works away on her books and articles and Prince Michael attends to business paperwork. Besides signed pictures of Queen Mary and Prince Michael's parents there is surprisingly a photograph of the American President Franklin D Roosevelt. The Prince, christened Michael George Charles Franklin, had the President as one of his godparents. The President's friendship with the Duke and Duchess of Kent was forged during a chance meeting when they were enjoying their honeymoon in the Bahamas.

Yet it is European rather than American influences which dominate the room. Their bookcase is filled with copies of classic authors such as Dickens, Shakespeare and Trollope, with a particular emphasis on Russian authors such as Dostoevesky and Tolstoy. Prince Michael, who has strong Russian roots and speaks the language fluently, is justifiably proud of his collection of rare Russian books – a legacy from Princess Marina and Prince Nicholas. Besides family heirlooms the Princess has books on interior design, art, cats, and horse riding. Paperback novels are out – Princess Michael has no place in her library for the kind of light romantic fiction favoured by Princess Diana.

It is in the study that the couple house their extensive collection of records. While one of the Princess's favourite records is 'Moon River' by Henry Mancini, her musical standards are rather more classical. Tchaikovsky, Beethoven, Mendelssohn, Vivaldi and Scarlatti are the mainstay of the couple's collection. While the Princess often talks about German opera, she listens to it rarely. She detests Wagner, even though the Queen once nicknamed her 'Our Val' because of her statuesque similarity to the German composer's Nordic heroines, the Valkyrie. Music after the 1890s is frowned upon and she has no room in her collection for the work of Benjamin Britten, William Walton or Gilbert and Sullivan. From

Prince William conducted his first royal inspection when he reviewed the Red Devils parachute display team, who literally dropped in on Kensington Palace

Off on an escapade in the park and getting too close to the water, Prince William is caught by his Scotland Yard bodyguard, who swings him away to safer ground

Would you recognise this woman? Wearing the traditional headscarf, Princess Diana does a little discreet shopping

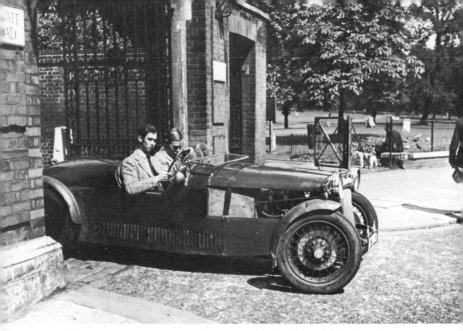

Prince Michael, aged 20 and already an expert driver, takes a friend for a spin around London in a borrowed car

Princess Michael signing copies of her first book, *Crowned in a Far Country*

Right: A white orchid given as a floral tribute by the Princess to her husband. The flower was plucked from a floral display at a fashion show held at the Victoria and Albert Museum

Below: Princess Michael shopping for furnishing fabrics

Lady Sarah Armstrong Jones and friends at Camberwell School of Art

Exhibiting motherly concern, Princess Margaret appears to be
having a stern word with her son, Viscount Linley

Princess Margaret in her drawing room

Above: The Earl of Ulster, Lady Rose Windsor (left) and Lady Davina Windsor, photographed on the back steps of their London home by Viscount Linley

Left: Riding his powerful Honda motorbike, the Duke of Gloucester is often mistaken for a bike messenger

the pop era, only the singer Neil Diamond passes the royal test of approval. She says: 'I live in the eighteenth century in my mind. I see my whole life as a cultivation of taste.'

Common to all the rooms in the house, the door to the study has a cat flap so that the Princess's array of Siamese and Burmese cats have the run of the house. She adores and pampers these beasts; nothing else divides her from the rest of the royal residents more than her love for these cats. Princess Margaret loathes them because their incessant howling and screaming at night keeps her awake. Prince Charles has given standing instructions that when they get into his kitchens – which is often during the summer – they should be physically kicked out. The Duchess of Gloucester throws them out of her garden because they terrorize her children's pet rabbit. Princess Michael's staff cannot abide the creatures and even mild-mannered Prince Michael rues the day he ever bought one as a wedding present.

The Princess's wedding gift, a jet-black Siamese called Kitty, was probably the most vicious of the lot. Before the Prince and Princess moved into Kensington Palace the wall at the bottom of their garden was used by nesting mallard ducks from the Serpentine. Traditionally, they would rear their baby ducklings here; when Princess Marina was alive she once helped a family of lost ducklings to find their mother on the other side of the wall. However, as soon as Kitty and her compatriot in crime, a Burmese called Magic, started their reign of terror the tradition quickly came to a bloody end. Within days the corpses of half-eaten ducklings littered the lawns or were dragged into the house and up to the couple's bedroom. One horrified witness said of Kitty: 'That animal is so vicious that I wouldn't be surprised if it attacked a sheep one day.' Her other cats are not quite so wild.

Often Prince Michael would wake up to the sound of crunching bones from the bottom of the bed, where the Princess's five cats slept. 'Do we have to sleep on top of an abattoir?' he asked angrily before storming out. Their staff often had the grisly job of removing the putrefying corpses of long-dead sparrows or pigeons from under the couple's king-size bed. For a woman of such taste and talent the Princess's cats represent her Achille's heel. They are allowed to climb up the curtains, scratch the antique furniture and rip the silk settees. As one bemused visitor said: 'I cannot understand the mentality that allows animals to undo so much good work.' But her cats are her life – she now has eight – and they rule every part of her routine. They appear at dinner to pick up scraps from under the table, they even feature in the nursery stories she tells her children. The Princess says: 'I have a Griselda story I tell. She is a witch I invented with a motorbike engine on her broomstick, and long black hair down to the floor with an orange stripe. She eats little fat children, her efforts are usually foiled by the magic cat, a Siamese.'

Nothing is too much for her pampered pets. They have their own marble slab by the side of the kitchen sink where a different flavour of pet food is placed in individual china dishes. When the couple entertain, the cats are fed left-overs of salmon and other treats. The Princess sends Christmas cards decorated with pictures of her cats.

When the Princess was the guest on the long-running radio programme, *Desert Island Discs*, she was asked what inanimate object she would want to take with her if she was marooned. The Princess wanted a cat – even though it broke the rules of the show. Her devotion to these animals truly knows no bounds. Once when she was on a private visit to America her favourite cat, Kitty, broke its back leg in a fall. It was taken to the vet and attended to. That evening the Princess telephoned home to see how things were going. She was told the children were well, the house was running smoothly but that Kitty had had an accident. The Princess was assured that she would be fine. Not so Marie-Christine. She was inconsolable until she saw Kitty again; she raced to the airport and caught the next plane home to nurse her 'darling Kitty'.

When Kitty went missing from her Nether Lypiatt home the Princess was heartbroken and offered a reward for its recovery. After she was discovered dead – a victim of a hit and run road accident – the Princess received two sacks of mail from wellwishers offering their sympathy. The residents and staff of Kensington Palace merely breathed a collective sigh of relief.

Another of her cats came to an equally sticky end in the grounds of Kensington Palace. During the spring the park-keepers go on a squirrel cull, using air rifles to thin out the population. It stops them damaging the young plants and triggering off the security systems which surround the private apartments. One day, however, they mistook one of Princess Michael's cats for a squirrel and inadvertently shot it. When they realized their mistake they dug a shallow grave for the animal, and never breathed a word to a soul about the incident for fear of attracting Princess Michael's wrath.

Her wrath is easy to attract. 'I am impatient,' she admits. Constant exercise is the one way she works off the frustrations of daily life; tennis in the summer, riding in the country, eurythmic classes every day. Like other royal couples, the Prince and Princess start their days at different times.

Prince Michael, a former major in the intelligence corps, is the early riser. For a while the couple used to get up at six in the morning and go out riding with the Household Cavalry through Hyde Park. That practice has now ended. Instead Prince Michael gets himself up at eight o'clock, after being woken by the alarm clock by the side of his bed. He eats alone in the dining room and every day has a slice of cold fresh tongue, a ripe tomato, a glass of orange juice and a glass of milk. While he flicks through *The Times* – the couple only take *The Times* and the *Daily Telegraph* – he opens the mail, which has been laid out by his place setting along with a paper knife. While he is downstairs eating his breakfast the Princess is upstairs savouring her cup of china tea in a huge Meissen breakfast cup. She eats a bowl of bran while she too goes through her mail, and browses through *The Times*. She says: 'I usually start with Bernard Levin's column; I am a great fan as well as a friend. Then I turn to the leaders and letters.'

In the early days, Prince Michael would don his motorbike leathers and kick his huge 500 cc Honda motorbike into life before heading off for his military job in Whitehall. Princess Michael often came down in her dressing gown, gave him a kiss and stood at the door to wave him off to work. Since he left the Army and took on a number of City directorships, including Standard Telephone and Cables, he travels to work

in a chauffeur-driven Jaguar. The Prince, as President of the
Royal Automobile Club, is a motoring fanatic, and the
garages at Kensington Palace have accommodated everything
from Ford Fiestas and Range Rovers, to a racy black Ford XR3
and the Jaguar.

When Prince Michael is safely off to work, the Princess
dresses and goes upstairs to the third floor nursery to see the
children – if they are at home. Since leaving Wetherby preparatory school, Lord Freddie goes to boarding school, while
Lady Ella attends a local school. If the truth be told, the
Princess feels as happy with her cats as her children, and
confesses: 'I rarely spend long stretches of time with the
children during the day but see them often for short times.'

After chatting to the children she wanders down to the
basement (the royal offices) to see her private secretary, currently Colonel Michael Farmer, to discuss invitations,
requests and general royal business. A number of the trickier
problems are referred to officials at Buckingham Palace for a
final yea or nay.

Around ten o'clock it is time for the Princess's private
exercise class. Her tutor arrives at the apartment and they
spend an hour each day in a stringent stretching routine to tone
up the muscles. The eurhythmic class also involves yoga and
meditation to help breathing and relax the body. In the warm
weather the Princess prefers to work out on the tennis court,
often travelling to Queen's at seven o'clock for a game with
the club pro. The Princess cuts quite a figure as she walks
down the drive dressed in her ankle-length white culottes.
After she has burnt off a few calories she likes to do a little
shopping, to see friends, or make a few telephone calls. Even
though she has her own office staff she is not above answering
the phone herself. But the way she does it displays her manic,
rather neurotic personality. When the phone rings she will
answer it and speak in a perfect English accent, posing as the
secretary. When the caller asks for the Princess she puts her
hand over the phone and then pretends to go and look. After a
couple of minutes she will speak again, this time as the Princess, but speaking with a German accent to emphasize her
foreign origins. By adopting these accents she tries to obscure

her Australian roots – she was brought up by her mother in Sydney – and emphasize her family's aristocratic European origins.

The Princess's royal status continually vexes her. When the highly respected royal author Christopher Warwick had the temerity to suggest in one book that she was a 'commoner' she summoned him to Kensington Palace and insisted that he change his text. On another occasion she sent a bag containing thirty pieces of silver to her former friend, the journalist and writer Jilly Cooper, after a newspaper profile which she considered unflattering. Jilly's husband Leo treated the snub lightly and put the money on a racehorse which romped home to victory.

Princess Michael is careful of her rank to the point of the ridiculous. When a fashionable interior designer sent her a Christmas card addressed to 'Princess Michael of Kent' she asked her private secretary to complain, saying that it should have been sent to 'Her Royal Highness Princess Michael of Kent'. Even long-standing friends must call her 'Ma'am' although occasionally she will relent. 'Yes, you *can* call me Marie-Christine,' she will say to close family friends after giving the matter serious consideration.

In the days when she could afford a chauffeur-cum-butler the Princess insisted that he put the red royal crown on the roof of the car, even if they were just popping out to the shops. Accepted practice is for these royal insignia to be used only for public engagements, not for private use. Even Prince Michael felt that she was abusing her position and asked her to remove the crown. She reluctantly obeyed but it did not prevent her ordering her chauffeur, Ian Armstrong, to turn on the interior lights when they were going to a semi-public duty at the Victoria and Albert Museum. 'I want people to see me, Ian,' she said. He did as he was asked but rattled through the traffic to get her to the museum as quickly as possible, to save his own embarrassment. His instincts were probably correct. The Princess seems to have an unhappy flair for attracting trouble. When she was driving to her tennis club one morning she was surrounded by a gang of youths who pulled faces at her and banged on the car when she was stopped at traffic lights. Even the drive into Kensington Palace is a hazard for her. Guests at the Royal Garden Hotel, which overlooks the drive, have the unnerving habit of dropping things from their balconies. On one occasion the Princess narrowly missed injury when a roller skate bounced on to the car's bonnet.

While the Princess likes to have her status confirmed with the general public – 'the peasants' as she prettily describes them – it is with the rest of the royal family that she really longs to be accepted. Nothing galls her more than the intractable royal pecking order that has her arrive the last. This happened when she was due to appear at the Chelsea Flower Show. The royal cars arrived and departed in reverse order. Princess Michael was forced to leave last even though she had a pressing appointment. There was nothing she could do but put on a brave face. However there was one delicious irony. While Princess Michael was waiting to leave, at least she was recognized and cheered by the crowd. The Duchess of Gloucester did not even have that consolation. Although she arrived and left before Princess Michael, few people were aware of her royal position and assumed she was a lady-in-waiting. The result was that the Duchess came away irritated and Princess Michael fuming – but neither royal rival would dream of discussing their discomfiture with each other. Oh the perils of public life.

It was during a similar royal procession after the Derby that Princess Michael again felt her status was not properly recognized. While the rest of the royals left in sleek Rolls Royces, the Michaels had to make do with a Jaguar. The Princess felt that because it was so low slung the crowds could not see her properly. She was determined to rectify the matter. Shortly afterwards the royal couple took possession of a beautiful Rolls Royce Phantom VI, which was a gift from an admiring friend. The fabulous present came during the height of her friendship with the American businessman, self-styled Baron Enrico di Portanova. He was lavish with his hospitality to the royal couple – even inviting them to his Acapulco home – and he is widely regarded as the mystery benefactor.

The royal couple enjoy the company of many charitable friends, from millionaire financier Peter de Savary who gave them a plot of land on the Caribbean island of Antigua, to Argentinian meat baron Carlos Perdomo who entertained the couple on his splended yacht *Jessica* at the height of the controversy surrounding Princess Michael's friendship with John Ward Hunt.

A high profile royal couple like the Michaels cannot live on charity and friendship alone, and there has been continuing controversy about how the royal couple make ends met. Marie-Christine admits: 'We do have to run a very tight ship. We manage. We sort of cope.' They employ a number of staff, enjoy two homes and a luxurious lifestyle, yet have an income of around £45,000 from his City directorships and her directorship of the Mayfair art dealers, MacConnal-Mason. The solution to the riddle lies behind the red brick walls of Kensington Palace. From time to time the royal couple will sell off pieces of Fabergé or pictures. One Impressionist painting by Boudin, which the couple sent to Christies for auction, raised around £15,000. Often the staff would spend the mornings with a ball of steel wool rubbing out the family crest from the solid silver cutlery and candlesticks so that it could not be traced. Then they put the treasures into a suitcase and took it to silversmiths in the backstreets of Bloomsbury. One former member of staff recalls: 'It brings me out in a sweat to think what we used to get up to, bringing back suitcases full of cash thrown in the back of a Range Rover. If we had ever been mugged goodness knows what would have happened.'

Yet while the royal couple have a high expenditure their day to day lifestyle is not particularly lavish. If Prince Michael can manage it he will drive home for lunch. Omelettes are a favourite or, for a change, lamb chops served with two vegetables. The couple rarely drink wine, preferring Perrier water or the occasional vodka and tonic. Yet while the Princess is fussy about food – her dinners usually begin with fish, followed by a meat course and dessert – she is not very worried about the wine. Prince Michael enjoys a good claret, the Princess a white burgundy. She turns her nose up at German or Loire Valley wine. The house is too small for their own wine cellar; when they have a dinner party they will slip down to Cullens wine merchants in the Kings Road, and buy a couple of cases. If Prince Michael is not available the Princess will invite one of her friends for an intimate lunch. Queen Noor is a regular guest. Once the Princess, who often hires extra staff from Buckingham Palace, borrowed a novice cook at short notice. The cook was so nervous that she spilt sticky hollandaise sauce over the butler. Queen Noor and the Princess did not bat an eyelid when the butler walked in to serve the meal covered in yellow goo.

After lunch, the Princess may go to the study to write, or work for her art company. Before she wrote her successful book *Crowned in a Far Country*, she had been toying with the idea of writing a biography of Elizabeth of Bohemia, a seventeenth-century monarch known as the Queen of Hearts. In addition to doing a little library research she had not got much further than copying pages out of other writer's books for her own notes. However, when she was commissioned by her friend, publisher George Weidenfeld, to write the lives of eight famous ladies who had become Queens in a foreign land, she tackled the task with a will. As she says: 'I used to be a very successful interior designer, but once I married Prince Michael I couldn't continue. What was there left for a mad princess to do decently? History seemed a safe subject.'

She used a word processor and a cut-and-paste method of operation, taking out chunks from fellow writer's books and wedging them in alongside her own words. Prince Michael corrected the spelling and took out some of the more risqué passages – which Princess Michael promptly restored – before the book was ready for publication. Although it reached the best seller list, the Princess had to pay out an agreed sum for plagiarizing the work of another author. In addition her television interviews to advertise the book merely earned her more bad publicity. The work was a labour of love and for three months she didn't ride or play tennis. She admits: 'My husband said my personality changed, I was unbearable, perfectly awful.'

When the pressure of work is not too much the Princess joins her daughter in the nursery for tea and occasionally stays with her during bathtime. Essentially however Princess Michael is an old-fashioned aristocrat who prefers to see her children when they are washed and dressed and looking 'perfectly angelic'. Prince Michael, who grew up without a father, will spend more time with the children, playing games and reading stories. Ella likes 'naughty stories' the best.

In the early days of parenthood both the Prince and Princess were hopelessly impractical when it came to dealing with their children. When Lord Freddie was a baby he was cared for by their nanny, Jean Rowcliffe, a sensible, no-nonsense Canadian girl. One evening the Princess allowed Jean to go out. Before leaving Jean plugged in the baby alarm in case the infant woke up. Shortly after she had left Lord Freddie woke up and started screaming. The Prince and Princess stood outside the nursery door not knowing quite what to do. Finally they worked themselves up into such a state that they contacted the Royal Protection Squad to ask them to find Jean. A search party was sent out and Nanny Rowcliffe dashed back to the apartment to comfort the sobbing child. 'It was rather pathetic really,' recalls one former member of staff. 'Here was this royal couple who just didn't have a clue about what to do with their own child.'

The Princess does like to show off her finery to her admiring daughter if she is going out to a ball or a banquet. She says: 'They haven't realized completely yet that I am not like other mummies. I was leaving for a fancy dress ball in a crinoline, tiara and with a Prince of Wales feather in my hair – frankly I felt like the sugar plum fairy. Ella said: "Mummy you look just like a Princess." "But Mummy is a Princess," I told her. My husband and I fell into each other's arms.'

However, the penalty of being a Princess was forcibly brought home to Marie-Christine one evening while she was watching the news in their kitchen. Normally their routine is to have a drink with their private secretary in the drawing room where they will discuss the day's business before having dinner. They regularly eat in the kitchen with paper napkins on the table, food from the fridge and the portable television switched on for the news. The couple were preparing for a State banquet at Windsor in honour of President Hastings Banda of Malawi when the BBC's *Six O'Clock News* came on. Princess Michael's father's Nazi past had been exposed in the newspapers that day and the Princess found to her horror that the television news was almost exclusively about that story. She says: 'Eighteen minutes were devoted to this story and showed old footage of Nazi atrocities. I was physically sick and the whole time my face was in cameo in the corner of the screen.' Prince Michael, who had disapproved of his wife appearing on *TV-am*, changed his mind after watching the drama played out quite literally by the kitchen sink.

It is the dramatic role that Princess Michael is best at playing. Nothing is quite so theatrical as when she plays the hostess for her glamorous dinner parties. The dramatis personae are internationally known figures from the world of showbusiness, politics and literature. Playwright Tom Stoppard, television presenter David Frost, humorist Alan Coren, politician Norman St John Stevas, Dr Roy Strong, the Director of the Victoria and Albert Museum, and Prime Minister Margaret Thatcher have all enjoyed the Michaels' hospitality. Marie-Christine has a soft spot for the Prime Minister. 'I'm mad about her. She doesn't waffle or witter. She is a strong powerful woman of great character.' Besides well-known public figures, her cast list is also peopled by those characters who flit in and out of international airports and newspaper gossip columns. Seriously rich Iranians, social-climbing American millionaires, all are welcomed to the feast. These guests often return her friendship by offering holidays and hospitality to the royal couple.

The Princess is undoubted mistress of ceremonies, while Prince Michael is content to play the role of chief mummer. He eats little and says less and normally throughout dinner faces a barrage of abuse from the supreme star of the show. 'Michael, fill up the guest's glasses.' 'Don't talk such rubbish.' 'You have been talking to the woman on your left for too long.' And so she rails on, a talent to amuse and abuse. Occasionally he fights back. At the time of various newspaper revelations about Princess Michael, residents were kept awake by a noisy row in Apartment 10. The next day workmen were called to carry away a chandelier for urgent repair. For the most part Prince Michael accepts her tirades with a smile, or a gentle wry joke.

Like Princess Diana, Marie-Christine loves to flirt with attractive men during dinner. She enjoys talking about sex almost as much as she does about money and she is not ashamed to push her husband's name forward for possible business deals. At the same time she is the most indiscreet member of the royal family, forever making sly allusions to her royal neighbours or to the newest member of the royal star list, the Duchess of York. 'A Coronation Street Princess,' she will say. 'The girl devalues the currency.'

Yet undoubtedly Princess Michael possesses magnetism, charisma that she can switch on in a way that is simultaneously unnerving and fascinating to both sexes. Her performances are rarely matched, let alone dwarfed, by those of other guests. However, during one dinner party the Princess did find a true equal in the shape of the legendary Hollywood star, Ava Gardner. The night Ava came to dinner she turned in an Oscar winning performance. She made her entrance in a flowing white evening gown with ostrich feathers touching the ground. From the moment she sipped her first scotch and soda she held the company spellbound with her anecdotes and humour. Halfway through dinner the loquacious lady decided that she needed to powder her nose. However she had taken off her snowy-white high heeled shoes during the meal and only found one. Mustering all her dignity, she rose imperiously and swayed and hopped across the room oblivious to the fact that she had one shoe on and one shoe off.

It was more of a melodrama than a comedy the night the Gloucesters reluctantly came to dinner. The curtain was due to rise at 8.15 pm sharp. The soufflé was in the oven, the rest of the guests were enjoying a pre-dinner drink in the drawing room. As the cheese soufflé rose, there was no sign of the Gloucesters. In nervous agitation Princess Michael went to the front door to peer out for them. Still no sign. It was touch and go with the soufflé. Fifteen minutes later the Gloucesters arrived from their home, which is about 300 yards away. Marie-Christine hissed at her butler: 'Don't give them a drink – bring them straight into dinner.' The soufflé was saved but the atmosphere was frozen throughout the meal. It did not warm up until the ladies retired to leave the men to their port and cigars. The Gloucesters, realizing that they had offended Princess Michael, stayed longer than was strictly necessary to try and sooth her ruffled feathers.

The Princess is a stickler for punctuality and keeping to a plan. One evening she organized a dinner party at Nether Lypiatt and had asked a Kensington Palace cook to prepare the pancakes beforehand for crêpes Suzette. Inadvertently they were left behind in London. The Princess refused to let her staff at Nether Lypiatt make any more. Instead she made her chauffeur drive the 150 miles back to London to pick them up. This is her style. To treat people, from her staff to her husband, with disdain one moment, charm the next. Rarely a week goes by without her dismissing someone, only to welcome them back hours later.

Since Princess Michael arrived on the royal stage she has taken over Princess Margaret's position as the black sheep of the family. Mean, moody and magnificent, Princess Michael truly fits the role of the many dazzling and domineering women who have dominated Kensington Palace throughout its history. She is never so happy as when she is turning a drama into a crisis, an argument into a showdown, a social slip into a personal outrage.

As the rest of the royal family have found, life with Marie-Christine is never boring. She has helped turn the pleasant backwater of Kensington Palace into a sea of stormy relations. When she first joined the royal troupe, this regal prima donna said a little prayer: 'Please God, don't let me make a gaffe.' Her prayers have rarely been answered.

5

The Theatrical Princess

Princess Margaret

It was the biggest night in the life of the young footman. He had been asked to help serve dinner to the Queen and Queen Mother at a dinner party hosted by Princess Margaret. Although nervous, the first two courses were served without incident. Then came the chef's *pièce de résistance* – crêpes Suzette flambéd at the table. In the kitchen another, more senior servant took several swigs of the brandy, pronounced with a grin that it had matured sufficiently, and then, with a flourish, lit the flame. Gingerly the young footman carried the flaming crêpes into the dining room and proceeded to serve the Queen. So far, so good. Then disaster struck. As he turned to serve Princess Margaret, who was sitting on the Queen's left, the fumes from the brandy, and the steam from the cooking crêpes, pricked his eyes. As he blinked vigorously he never noticed that he was standing on the Princess's dress. In a blur of movement, his foot slipped, the silver tray dipped and a waterfall of flaming brandy cascaded down her gown.

The Queen watched this extraordinary scene with a quizzical expression and then in a voice of calm glee said to the Queen Mother: 'Oh look Mummy, Margo is on fire,' as though it were the most natural thing in the world. The footman, aghast at his blunder, set down the tray and tried to damp the flames with his hands. This act lasted but a moment until he realized he was committing something akin to *lèse-majesté* as he tried to pat out the flames on the burning bodice. He ran out in confusion while another servant doused the flames with a spare napkin. All the while the Queen and Queen Mother looked on calmly without raising a finger to help. They obviously felt it was part of the entertainment.

After much coaxing the shame-faced youth was prevailed upon to serve the coffee. When he returned not one member of the royal party batted an eyelid. The lad went to bed that night amazed both that he still had his job and at the sang-froid of the royal family.

While the incident was not planned, the Queen and Queen Mother could be forgiven for thinking that it was entirely in character. Princess Margaret's life is something of a theatrical event. She loves nothing more than to turn the routine into the extraordinary, to amuse with a surprise, to add a little gilt to the gingerbread of life.

The fashionable image of Princess Margaret is the tragic, sad and lonely princess living off her memories. The truth is rather different. Of course she has experienced disappointment, heartbreak and serious illness, but as she enters late middle age she has a regal calm and an amused yet interested view of the world that is reflected in her life at Number 1A, Clock Court, Kensington Palace. A close friend says: 'People say she is a sad person. But that's such a cliché. She has a rather nice life, very merry, warm and giving. Her house has a life-giving atmosphere about it. There is always something going on.'

The Princess herself admits she has changed. 'My friends used to tease me and say that I had got my acid drop expression,' she says. 'That doesn't happen a lot now though. I'm much nicer in my old age.'

Having taken the high fences – and not a few falls – in life she is now enjoying the canter along the flat. There is still plenty of room for fun and excitement even at her present pace. She appeared on the long-running radio show *The Archers,* playing herself, and was thrilled when she was hauled aloft on a stage cloud during a private party at Covent Garden opera house.

Princess Margaret delights in the unusual, the off-beat. One evening she walked out of her apartment in the costume of Marie Antoinette. She was on her way to a society fancy dress ball. The Princess spotted a student botanist who was working in the palace for the summer. She called him over. 'Do you like it?' she asked mischievously. Then she did an elegant twirl, her crinoline gown swirling over the cobbled courtyard. The student made suitable appreciative noises, then as she was about to get into her limousine she held out the cake she was carrying. 'Let them try and eat that,' she said, aping Marie Antoinette's original phrase. 'It's made of plastic.'

Her sense of the dramatic was on display too when she invited the Queen and Prince Philip to supper to celebrate his birthday. When the royal party, who had been to the theatre, arrived back at her apartment she got her duty staff together – butler John Leishman, chef Stan Wasneiski and housekeeper Liz Greenfield – and lined them up in the stone-flagged entrance hall. As Prince Philip walked in they broke into a ragged, if slightly embarrassed, chorus of 'Happy Birthday'. The Prince rocked back on his heels with merriment at the absurdity of it all.

The theatricality of life upstairs – Margaret's friends are drawn from the world of theatre, ballet and other arts – is mirrored downstairs. Her chef, one of the Palace's real characters, has three grown sons, all of whom he has named after film stars. They are Marlon, after Marlon Brando, Tyrone, after Tyrone Power, and Gary, after Gary Cooper.

It was film-star glamour that Princess Margaret and her husband Anthony Armstrong-Jones brought to Kensington Palace when they moved in nearly thirty years ago. They settled into Apartment 10 when they first arrived in the autumn of 1960. Just as the Kennedys had brought intellectual style and drive to Washington, so this royal couple reflected the new atmosphere of Swinging London. They had flair, style, artistic temperaments and a galaxy of well-known friends. It appeared that Kensington Palace would become a revived centre for the arts and patronage of the arts. Yet while they cleared away a few cobwebs surrounding the royal family, they never managed to thoroughly spring clean the institution. The couple had too many private problems – Armstrong-Jones fitting in with royal life and Princess Margaret coping with a new house and burgeoning family – to generate fundamental changes. Royal author John Pearson is being too harsh, however, when he says that their 'failure' was a major missed opportunity of the reign. With internationally-known figures such as Noel Coward, Cecil Beaton and Peter

Sellers breathing new life into Kensington Palace during their
regular visits, the Snowdons did force the pace of change
within the royal circle.

Certainly their creativity was superbly expressed in their
second home at Kensington Palace. Yet complaints about the
cost of refurbishment detracted from the work they put into a
decayed ruin of a building. The decision to move apartments
was taken because their first home, 'the doll's house', proved
too small for the amount of entertaining they were expected to
undertake.

The Government spent £80,000 – 'enough to rehouse sixteen homeless families' complained one outraged Member of
Parliament – for the task of renovating a property that had
been unoccupied ever since the death of Princess Louise in
1939. Much of the rambling apartment had not been decorated
since Queen Victoria's day. It presented a gloomy sight to the
new occupants. It is a measure of their success that visitors are
impressed by the overall feel of the house. 'The place is like a
country house in the middle of town,' said one guest. 'You
fully expect golden labradors to come bounding at you when
you walk inside.'

The Romanesque entrance hall, flagged with black and
white Welsh stone, is dominated by an Annigoni oil painting
of the Princess. It leads off to Princess Margaret's favourite
room, the drawing room. This is the largest room in the
twenty room apartment and is both regal and informal, an
effect achieved by the peacock blue colour scheme and the
Princess's natural untidiness. Papers are scattered around her
desk, half-eaten boxes of chocolates hidden by armchairs. The
Princess was brought up in large rooms and she claims that she
always heads for the largest room in any house.

Princess Margaret chooses her own fabrics and one of the
few things she and Princess Michael of Kent have in common
is their love of Fortuny's fabrics. The highly polished wooden
doors veneered by the Snowdons themselves are always kept
shut. Ever since childhood Princess Margaret has hated sitting
in draughty open rooms. The patterned carpet, a mixture of
subdued gold, blue and orange was a wedding present from
the City of London; it was made in Spain and designed by her

theatrical friend Carl Toms. Around the fireplaces are powder blue and gold settees that match the carpet. However, Princess Margaret finds that while the chairs are comfortable many friends prefer sitting about on the floor. 'I like that,' she says, 'it shows they feel at home here.' When guests remark that her home looks like an eighteenth-century mansion the Princess will nod in agreement. 'Well, it was built by Wren,' she says. 'It is in character.'

Dominating the room is the baby grand piano given as a wedding present by the Count and Countess of Rosse. Its lacquered lid is covered with family photographs – the Queen and Prince Philip after the Coronation, Prince Charles and Princess Anne as children, Viscount Linley and Lady Sarah Armstrong-Jones in their school uniforms. The most unusual picture is a witty photograph of the Queen Mother deliberately hiding her diamond tiara with a silk scarf.

Against the library walls stands a superb six-panelled mahogany breakfront cabinet housing a collection of porcelain, while at the entrance to the dining room two glistening blackamoor figures stand guard. In the ground floor garden room (which used to be the guard room) there are reminders of her other home, her cliff-top mansion, Les Jolies Eaux, on the Caribbean island of Mustique. Here she houses her superb collection of sea shells which experts from the Natural History Museum regard as one of the finest in private ownership.

Seashells and blue glass form the theme throughout her apartment at Kensington Palace. In her bathroom, complete with sunken bath and gold and white Greek pillars, she has a six-sided glass towel rail which houses more shells. Her bedroom has shells laid out on a glass-top table near her pink three-quarter size bed. Blue glassware, the colour of lapis lazuli, stands on the shelves. This decoration is amplified in the sandy-coloured dining room. This ground floor room, which overlooks Princess Margaret's cherished magnolia tree in the large grassed garden, is decorated with John Piper's figurative paintings of Venice. The polished oval table, which can seat fourteen, is usually set for two at lunch – normally the Princess and a lady-in-waiting. For a typical lunch a bottle of Californian Chablis will be chilling in the corner, a bottle of red waiting in the wings. At the Princess's place setting there are two blue glasses, an unopened bottle of Malvern water and a bell – naturally in the shape of a shell – to summon her butler. Her current passion for blue glassware has meant that much of her clear Scottish crystal has been stored in the butler's pantry. When she is away at weekends, or in winter, in Mustique, her entire glass and shell collections are painstakingly dusted and washed. Just as painstaking has been the cataloguing of her book collection in the ground floor library, formerly Lord Snowdon's study. She has collected some 12,000 books during her life, mostly on travel, ballet, art and literature. The works of Iris Murdoch and Doris Lessing rather than Jackie Collins grace her shelves. Like the rest of the house the library has a lived-in feeling, slightly battered and dated yet restful and serene; a home where a bright red fire extinguisher leans against an elegant George Morrison grandfather clock and where the sonorous ticking of the English bracket clock in the dining room gives you a feeling of quiet repose. In fact repose is the atmosphere in the house until late morning. In contrast to the rest of the royal family (except the Queen Mother) Princess Margaret is notoriously late to bed and late to rise.

The Princess's day starts very quietly at eleven o'clock when her jolly housekeeper, Liz Greenfield, takes up a tray of tea – Lapsong Suchong served in Spode china – to her bedroom. After she has dressed and read her mail she will call for a cup of very strong black Brazilian blend coffee. She takes it everywhere with her. When she travels on a Queen's flight a silver flask of her favourite coffee from the Nairobi Coffee Company goes with her.

There is no rigid pattern to her day. In the late morning she may go out with a friend to watch a ballet rehearsal, meet her private secretary to discuss any royal business or spend an hour shopping. Her secretary, Muriel Murray-Brown, spends much of the morning organizing guests for lunch.

Every Monday Princess Margaret goes through the week's menu. Her menu card, printed at Buckingham Palace, offers her a similar choice to that presented to the Queen and the Queen Mother. She does not have a large appetite – 'People don't like me fat,' she says – but she is an epicure. Unlike

Prince Philip who simply shovels his food down without much thought about what he is eating, Princess Margaret likes to consider her menus and has an extensive knowledge of international dishes. However she is a patriotic diner. Where possible everything must be British: English raspberries, Scotch salmon, English lamb, Scotch beef, venison and game from the royal estates. Asparagus is her favourite starter, she loves fillet of beef cooked rare, any kind of shellfish and of course smoked salmon. Like her father George VI she prefers her bacon crisp and smokey. Like the Queen Mother she prefers her liver finely sliced. Her pet dislikes are any kind of fruit with meat, such as duck à l'orange. One day, to keep her chef on his toes, she wrote in her menu book 'haddock Monte Carlo' next to the space provided for Friday lunch. Her chef had never heard of the dish. But he refused to admit defeat and ask her for the recipe. He spent days going through library books until finally he tracked the recipe down in a Victorian cook book. It is in fact a very sophisticated kedgeree. Another favourite is Eggs Ville Roi, a tasty dish which she enjoys as a starter.

The Princess's staple luncheon fare is boiled chicken, potatoes and vegetables (she enjoys mange tout and fennel). It is served between one and half-past one and unless Princess Margaret's secretary finds a guest in the morning's phone-round she will eat with a lady-in-waiting. Princess Margaret, who hates eating on her own, often dines with the Queen Mother. Indeed Princess Margaret and the Queen Mother spend most weekends together at the Royal Lodge at Windsor. Her former lover Roddy Llewellyn, who still does her garden, visits every so often, as does Lord Snowdon who only lives half a mile away. These are informal, intimate affairs, although the Princess will often annoy her guests by picking at her food while imploring them to 'eat up'.

This peacefully civilized atmosphere was severely strained the day Nancy Reagan came to lunch. She swept up the drive in a bombproof black Cadillac, the weight of a double-decker bus, followed by a small army of armed Secret Service agents. The 'deaf men' – so called because they communicate by talking into a microphone in their sleeves connected to an electronic earpiece – swarmed over the house. They eyed the royal staff suspiciously, sniffing the game pie before it was served as though it was an unexploded bomb. The industrially designed kitchen is large enough to take a bank of three electric ovens bedded in green Welsh slate. But that day the weight of numbers cramped the Polish chef's style.

It was the chef himself who cramped Prince Andrew's style the day the Prince came to visit the kitchens. Andrew, who was then romancing the American actress Koo Stark, took a fancy to a young assistant cook called Hilary. In fact the Prince had quite a fondness for staff during his bachelor days. He once enjoyed a rather saucy water pistol fight with an attractive blonde nanny employed by the Gloucesters. On this occasion even his warm playboy charm and tales of life in the navy could not cut any ice. The young lady was impervious to his wiles, and during the hour he spent chatting her up she stayed close to the Polish chef, busying herself with kitchen chores. At the 1986 Christmas staff party at Buckingham Palace where all the royal family mingle with those who serve them, Prince Andrew was reminded of his romantic failure. He remembered the incident and quickly put his finger to his lips. 'Ssh, don't say a word, the wife is just behind me,' he joked, referring to the Duchess of York.

After lunch Princess Margaret, who has between three and four engagements a week, is usually on duty, sweeping down the drive with her motorcycle escort, the 'Black Rats'. When she is not working she likes to pore over her official papers and fill in her leather-bound diary, which she has kept consistently for most of her colourful life. Like the Queen, she relaxes by solving intricate jigsaw puzzles. It is a talent that mesmerised former Labour Minister Richard Crossman when he visited Sandringham. In his diary he noted that she could talk to guests while quietly fitting in pieces at the same time.

In the summer the Princess has fun by taking her friends on picnics to the royal parks. Once Prince Edward accompanied her daughter Sarah when the royal party set out for Kew Gardens. Princess Margaret travelled in style, taking her butler and chef along to organize and serve the food. While the party enjoyed the sunshine, her chef was on the floor of the

Queen's House looking for a power point for the electric toaster. No royal picnic is complete without hot buttered toast and pâté.

Whenever there is a hint of a warm day the Princess heads for her white wrought-iron terrace – 'My eighteen feet of Mustique' she calls the verandah which overlooks her walled garden. She eats lunch here and sunbathes when it is hot enough. While the scent from the roses wafts in on the afternoon breeze, her reveries are often upset by the sight of onlookers from the Royal Garden Hotel peering into her private paradise. Her garden is her pride and joy. At one acre it is the largest of the royal gardens, complete with magnolia trees, camelias and rose beds. There is even a mirrored arch at the bottom to give the visitor the illusion that he can join the public park. Conscientiously the Princess will sponge down the leaves of her camellia bush to help it survive. However most of the hard work is down by two gardeners who come once a week to keep it in shape.

The garden is lovely in summer and it is here that she invites her friends to take afternoon tea. Like the rest of the royal ladies Princess Margaret makes it quite a little ceremony. Toasted sandwiches are regularly requested although she does have some unusual teatime fads. One afternoon she asked for digestive biscuits with marmalade. Like Prince Philip, who loves his barbeques, Princess Margaret enjoys eating al fresco – if it is properly done. In the evening when she goes to Covent Garden or to the theatre she will have a picnic supper prepared. Then in the interval her butler serves up the feast from a silver tray as the Princess and her guests chat in the royal box.

All of this is part of her ability to treat every aspect of life as an event. She will go out of her way to dress up for a dinner party because she feels it invests it with a sense of style. She says: 'In the evening in private life I'm very unfashionable in that I wear long dresses. People no longer seem to have a sense of occasion. My feeling is that if you're going out in the evening then you want to have a bath and change into clean clothes – you choose something to suit the occasion. To me, smartness is not only to do with clothes but make-up, hair, bags, jewellry, even nails. They all add up to the finished effect.'

She frequently hosts dinner parties and gives the same attention to the table decoration as she does to her own appearance. Hand cut red roses – her favourite flowers – adorn the table and the Princess makes sure each place setting has an onyx cigarette lighter and ashtray. When one famous television personality started fiddling with one of these expensive lighters the Princess spotted him, and, with a twinkle in her eye, said: 'Put that down. I'm not having you steal my things.' She is a generous hostess – 'Her bar has more drink than the Dorchester,' one guest noted with approval – although this does put a strain on her staff. Often she will announce at the last minute that the numbers for dinner have been increased because she has invited additional friends on a whim. Many is the time that her chef has run out of some ingredient or other and had to scuttle down to a late-night store on Kensington High Street for extra supplies. Other royal chefs are amazed at his versatility. 'I've seen him with a pan of vegetables one minute and then half an hour later turn it into an inspired concoction,' says one. 'But then again he has the Princess as a boss.'

The late Danny Kaye was a regular guest – he spoke better Polish than Princess Margaret's chef – and Princess Margaret was greatly saddened by his loss. Irish businessman and raconteur Ned Ryan is a frequent visitor, as is Carl Toms, Dame Margot Fonteyn, Rudolph Nureyev, and friends from the aristocracy such as Lord and Lady Glenconner (who gave her the plot of land on Mustique for a wedding present), Lord and Lady Buckhurst and banker Oliver Baring and his wife Veronica. When the Princess invited the tough characters from the television series *The Professionals* for dinner her staff fully expected them to come bursting through the door or crashing through the windows. Instead Bodie, Doyle and company put on their best evening suits and arrived in separate hired limousines.

The Princess enjoys the company of others, and it is a rare night indeed that she dines in alone. When that happens she eats from a tray and watches television. Even then she likes to have people around her. One evening while watching the film *Superman* she saw with delight that some of the many places she had visited were featured. She summoned her long-serving, and long-suffering, butler John Leishman to share her enjoyment. While she sat watching the film, pointing out places of interest, he was forced to stand there and make polite conversation. He was itching to sit down but could only do so when she commanded it. The command was never given.

Thankfully however the Princess is invariably out in the evening. She stays out so late that she is the only member of the royal family to carry a front door key, but she is always losing them. At home she enjoys hosting a formal dinner party. Asparagus or salmon are usually served first, with fillet of beef for the main course followed by a cold dessert. Before one dinner party where the entertainers John Dankworth and Cleo Laine were guests of honour, Dankworth's secretary rang to inform the Princess that he was vegetarian and that he could not eat any meat. Princess Margaret saw red; she would not be dictated to. Meat, and lots of it, was featured on the menu that night.

Depending on the company, the Princess plays party games such as Consequences after dinner, but normally loves to lead a sing-song. Her extensive record collection of jazz and twentieth-century American musicals reflects her own passions. She knows all the lyrics of *Showboat*, *Guys and Dolls* and *South Pacific* and will sit at the piano while she serenades her guests, wreathed in cigarette smoke and a glass of Famous Grouse whisky to hand. 'She has an incredible memory for lyrics,' says one loyal friend. 'These singalongs are great fun.'

Another friend, author Pat Booth, has a more unkind verdict of her royal performance. In a novel called *Palm Beach* Pat, who was a frequent guest at Kensington Palace, gave the following description: 'The voice was deep and throaty, the legacy of too many cigarettes, the hint, perhaps, of the odd late night. She wrapped her full, ripe lips indulgently round the syllables, milking them of their humour, as she rolled her eyes towards the ceiling.'

'Her voice was surprisingly, almost disturbingly deep – a bit like Betty Bacall on a bad day – and it tended to wander around like a leaf on the Chicago streets when it went for the higher notes. The accompaniment was standard saloon strum, the left hand pumping backward and forward. There were missed notes and missed words.'

'Her turretlike eyes swirled and swivelled to identify who was with her, who against her.'

'On the top of the battered black piano stood the glass of "Famous Grouse", the ashtray with its cargo of long cigarette holder and wispy burning cigarette.'

As her rendition continues one character is moved to comment: 'I think she'd really have liked to have a night club act. In fact, in a way I guess she is.'

As a night club singer *manqué* the Princess loves nothing more than to sit chatting and singing until the small hours. This does not please all the guests, who know that they cannot slink away before the royal assent has been given. At country house parties where the Queen is present, regulars know that the trick is to leave when the Queen retires, normally about eleven o'clock, as otherwise they will be trapped for several more hours. The servants however do have to wait around for guests to leave. One servant had a rather drastic solution to the problem of the royal night owl. During the course of the evening he had managed to consume an abnormal amount of alcoholic refreshment. The clock chimed two, then three and there was no sign of Princess Margaret nor her handful of guests retiring for the night. Finally the servant had had enough. Like an irritable restauranteur waiting to shut up shop, he simply switched off all the lights and stopped the conversation in mid flow. Princess Margaret called out from the gloom: 'I gather from that act that you want me to go.' The servant slurred back: 'Yes, ma'am,' and that was the end of the matter. Princess Margaret shrugged her shoulders and went off to bed after bidding an ironic 'goodnight' to the servant.

Yet Princess Margaret's staff are the most loyal and long serving of all the royal households within Kensington Palace. She mothers them, clucking round them like a hen to make sure that they are alright. Her butler, a gentle, softly spoken Scot from Falkirk, has been with her for twelve years. Theirs is a love-hate relationship but neither could do without the other. Her secretary has been with her for twenty years; she has a crippled mother and the Princess arranged for them to have a flat at Kensington Palace. When the chef's marriage broke up the Princess flew him to Balmoral during the summer holiday to give him a break. He faced further problems when he had to go into hospital for open heart surgery. On the eve of the operation the Princess rang with a few very private words of encouragement. She is the only royal who will regularly join in the fun below stairs. Whenever there is a big horse race she takes part in the staff sweepstake. In one Grand National she drew the winner and received ten pounds for her fifty pence stake.

While the staff know where they are with Princess Margaret, her son Viscount Linley does not inspire the same warmth. He has moved out of his room on the second floor but still visits regularly, as does his sister Sarah. He delights in 'winding up' John, the butler, who is a nervy character at the best of times. His favourite trick is to ring the front door bell and then go in through the kitchen entrance. As one Kensington Palace servant says: 'When Linley is around John has to take his pills.' He and Sarah were just as bad as children. They would often hide in Police Lodge so that Nanny Sumner could not find them. Princess Margaret's son has also annoyed the Royal Protection police with his daredevil antics. One of his frequent tricks was to ride his powerful BMW motorbike down the drive so that he could beat the security barrier before it came down. Once he roared down millionaire's row – the diplomatic quarter that runs parallel to Kensington Palace – so fast that the police warned him that he would be prosecuted if he did it again. Ironically, when Linley was a youngster, Princess Margaret insisted that signs saying 'Please drive carefully, children' were erected near the drive to help safeguard her family.

There was little improvement when Viscount Linley bought himself a black Ford Escort XR3. He came home late at night with the stereo blaring so loudly that it woke the Duke and Duchess of Gloucesters' children. They rang up to complain and Linley earned himself another black mark.

He lavished a lot of attention on his car and would let no one but himself clean it. One day a servant was walking by as he was putting the finishing touches to his vehicle with a wash leather. Just to pass the time of day the servant commented: 'I bet it will rain now you have washed it.' Linley gave him a blank look. 'Are you talking to me?' he replied. 'Yes,' said the servant. 'Call me sir,' said Linley abruptly and started cleaning his car again. 'Come the revolution,' muttered the servant as he went on his way, smarting from the insult.

As with all members of the royal family, servants soon realize they have to stand up to them or else they will be trampled on. One evening Princess Margaret's chef came home late to find Linley and his friends larking about in his spotless kitchen. Stan, who fought in World War II, was not having any of it and went into battle, angrily ordering Linley to clean up the mess. Shamefaced, he and his friends got to work.

Linley, who has inherited his father's rebellious streak, staged one of his more daring stunts within Kensington Palace. The curly-haired young man, who once turned up at a theatre in Bath dressed only in cowboy boots and overcoat, climbed on to the roof of Kensington Palace for a dare. Unlike Prince Philip, who was seen by the police when he tried a similar stunt during his youth, David Linley was never spotted. His escapade seventy feet above the ground in the pitch dark escaped detection by either patrolling policemen or the sophisticated alarm system.

While Linley gets mixed reviews from Kensington Palace staff, his sister Sarah is universally popular. 'Morning sunshine' is her normal cheery greeting to one and all. Although she moved into a house of her own in 1985 she sees her mother regularly. Sarah, an art student who is not too grand to visit secondhand clothes shops for her wardrobe, often comes up 'on the scrounge'. Like most students she has little spare cash and raids her mother's fridge and larder for food for her Fulham home.

With a house to furnish she also rummages around in the upstairs rooms for spare crockery and other useful knick-knacks. She is genuinely close to both parents and spends much time flitting between their houses. Her father Lord Snowdon says: 'Sarah spends a lot of time in and around the house. We talk about life and this and that.'

It is a relief to both parents that since their divorce, they have remained on good terms both with their children and with each other. While the break up was at times acrimonious – Snowdon would sit alone in his Kensington Palace study sipping claret, while Princess Margaret fretted in the drawing room – they have tried to forgive and forget.

When Princess Margaret returned home from a recuperative holiday in Mustique following her lung operation it was Sarah who was her first visitor. She had a light lunch with her mother and then Princess Margaret spent the rest of the day in bed. While Sarah visits often she always makes herself scarce if Roddy Llewellyn is around. There is no love lost between them. Roddy, who enjoyed a much publicized romance with Princess Margaret, still advises the Princess on her garden and visits about once a month, sometimes bringing his wife for lunch.

It was this relationship that brought Princess Margaret into conflict with the Queen, the Queen Mother and Prince Philip. They deeply objected to the way she was making a public spectacle of herself over a young man twenty years her junior. Since she dropped him she has become much closer to the Queen, especially since her lung operation. They frequently spend weekends together on the Queen's estate at Sandringham in Norfolk where they will stay in a cosy little house called Wood Farm.

During the difficult and depressing period following her operation when there was concern that Princess Margaret might have cancer, her royal neighbours rallied around. When she was too ill to perform a royal engagement in Wales, Princess Diana volunteered. She wandered over to Princess Margaret's apartment to see how she was and to be briefed on who she was meeting and what to watch for.

Margaret's relations with Diana are cordial – they have a mutual love of ballet – and she and Prince Charles will be invited to dine several times a year. When Prince Harry was born the Princess was one of Diana's first visitors. She took her friend, publisher Norman Lonsdale, along to Apartments 8 and 9 as well. Yet for some reason she left the urbane publisher kicking his heels in the Wales's waiting room for an hour while she cooed over the third in line to the Throne.

While she is friendly with Princess Diana, Princess Margaret will not hesitate to criticize the most glamorous member of the royal family when she is seen to step out of line. When Diana wore her hair in an unbecoming chignon style for the State Opening of Parliament, Princess Margaret and Prince Philip were furious. Diana's new look completely stole the Queen's thunder and while the Queen was unperturbed, Prince Philip and Princess Margaret felt that she had been upstaged. The final insult was when *The Times* referred to the Princess of Wales first and the Queen second in its report. When Princess Margaret met the Queen socially at a private party a few days later she made it clear that she felt Diana's behaviour was nothing more than a headline grabbing exercise, and one that had succeeded only too well. It was one of the Princess's first public engagements following the birth of Prince Harry and she was determined to make her mark again. Margaret was unimpressed. 'She has made a fool of you,' she told her sister frankly. Diana has not repeated that scene stealing style again.

In fairness, it must be said that Margaret's outburst was more to protect the Queen's image than out of any deep animosity for Diana.

The royal couple who have never offended by their headline stealing antics are Princess Margaret's next-door neighbours, the Duke and Duchess of Gloucester. She thinks that this retiring couple are 'sweet' and has them around for dinner from time to time.

Following Princess Margaret's operation the Gloucesters would take her with them to banquets in their royal car so that she would not have to travel on her own. But while they live cheek by jowl – the Princess can hear the Gloucester's children running along a corridor that crosses her apartment – day to day contact is minimal. As the Duke of Gloucester says: 'It's only rarely that we'd invite each other to dinner because we meet on so many other occasions. I've no idea where Princess

Margaret is now for example. Possibly if our chauffeur were sick we might borrow her chauffeur, or vice versa. We "lend a cup of sugar" so to speak.'

Occasionally Princess Margaret will see her other neighbour, the Queen Mother's cousin Lady Mary Clayton, across the courtyard. However she is always keen to muzzle the myth that she saw her governess, Marion Crawford, when she retired to the nearby Nottingham Cottage. 'Crawfie', who earned the abiding contempt of the royal family for selling her sugary sweet memoirs of her days with the two Princesses, boasted that Princess Margaret was a regular visitor to her rose-decked cottage. 'I never did,' explodes the Princess crossly when she is asked.

As for the Michaels, well, they could live on Mars for all the Princess sees of them, although she likes to keep up to date with the latest 'outrage' perpetrated by Princess Michael. It merely confirms her already low opinion. In common with the other royals, Princess Margaret watches the actions of her peers closely. Yet she has her own social set, her own daily routine. On important occasions she will invite all the royal family to her home, but these are rare. The last time was when Viscount Linley celebrated his twenty-first birthday, and the party went on until the small hours. Then Prince Charles and Princess Diana tucked in to the Beef Wellington, even though they were vegetarians.

For the most part Princess Margaret leads her own life, goes her own way. For years she was cast as the tragic character in the royal drama: now she is happy with her walk-on role. Her sense of the theatrical is still as great but these days she is happiest enjoying herself in private rather than causing dramas on the front pages.

6

The Reluctant Royals

The Duke and Duchess of Gloucester

The leather-clad figure of a motorbike rider roared up the drive towards the black and yellow security gate at the entrance to Kensington Palace. It was clear from his speed that the motorcyclist fully expected the gates to rise to allow him to ride on. They did not. The rider came to a hasty halt as a uniformed policeman emerged from his glassed-in shelter to verify the rider's identity. As his heavy bike stopped the anonymous rider forgot to put his feet down to steady himself. Like a scene from a Charlie Chaplin film, the bike slowly toppled on its side leaving the rider in a heap of leathers and confusion on the ground. Another day, another inauspicious entrance for the Duke of Gloucester.

He is destined to play the role of the public figure who people see in the street and say to themselves: 'I've seen that face before. Now what's his name?' Even when he wants to get into his own home, his anonymity has as many drawbacks as advantages. He says: 'When we first came here, there were four policemen we knew fairly intimately. Now that the Prince and Princess of Wales live here, there are I don't know how many, and they don't all know me, which is irritating when you try to get in and they say "Who are you?"'

With his owlish spectacles, podgy figure and dishevelled air of perpetual bafflement, the Duke of Gloucester gives the impression of being the brainiest but the most absent-minded boy in school.

He is a character destined for life in the ranks, not the front line. Yet family misfortune has thrust Richard, Duke of Gloucester, the second son of Henry, and his attractive Danish born wife Birgitte into the limelight.

His elder brother William, a career civil servant and something of a royal playboy, was killed while taking part in an air race in 1972. When his father died two years later Richard took the title and abandoned hopes for a quiet life as an architect. He went to Magdalen Collage, Cambridge, where he was known as Proggie to his friends (PROG – Prince Richard of Gloucester). Nowadays his nicknames are DOG (Duke of Gloucester) or Snappers, because of his love of photography.

On his second day at Cambridge Richard met a shy nineteen-year-old Danish secretary, Birgitte Eva van Deurs. In her father's words she was 'not beautiful, but very nice looking and very well educated.' Birgitte (pronounced 'big eater') liked Richard for his personality. 'He has a very good sense of humour,' she says.

Their wedding, on 8 July 1972, was quiet (just fifty guests). It took place at the local parish church in Barnwell, Northamptonshire, where Prince Richard's parents owned a 2500 acre estate. Birgette arranged the church flowers herself and typically invited six pensioners from the village almshouse to the ceremony, along with the Queen Mother, Prince Charles and Princess Margaret.

In the meantime Richard set up Hunt Thompson Associates in Camden, north London, with two fellow architects, Bernard Hunt and John Thompson. He cycled to work or arrived on his motorbike, put 'Richard Gloucester' on his business cards and tackled conversions for local authorities. The newly-weds were hoping to set up home in a converted warehouse in Rotherhithe in London's dockland when, six weeks after the wedding, Prince William was killed.

In 1974, on the death of his father, the third son of King George V, Richard assumed the title of Duke of Gloucester and inherited the Barnwell estate. Shortly before the Duke died he moved from York House in St James's Palace where the family had been living, to the more grandiose setting of Apartment 4, Kensington Palace, next door to Princess Margaret. The new Duke then took on the apartment. He says: 'When we came here we at last found a small, compact and charming house with a garden. My wife has redecorated several of the rooms. It's her nest so to speak.'

While thrust into the world of public affairs – between them they are patrons of some seventy organizations – the Duke and Duchess succeed in leading a quiet, family life. But like all royals they have their quirks and eccentricities.

During the week they stay at Kensington Palace together with the Duke's mother, Princess Alice, Duchess of Glouces- ter, where she has a small suite of rooms. At the weekend they all pile into their white Citroën estate and head off for Barn- well. At Kensington Palace the Duchess rules the roost; at Barnwell it is Princess Alice who is mistress.

However it is their three children, Alexander, the Earl of Ulster, Lady Davina and Lady Rose who totally dominate their lives and homes. Unlike the Wales's children, they have complete freedom to roam where they wish. In the entrance hall there are bikes, balls and roller skates to greet the visitor. 'Sometimes one feels as if one is working in a crèche,' says their private secretary, Sir Simon Bland. Unlike the Kents and the Wales, the Gloucesters do not ban their children from their bedroom nor do they put them on a separate floor. They all sleep in the same quarters, the two girls sharing a bedroom. Normally they are awake at any time from five in the morning and go running into their parents. On the rare occasions they sleep in, the Gloucesters are as likely to be woken by the sound of Moslem children playing in the public park during Ramadan. Then the children of the diplomats are woken before dawn and because they don't want to go back to bed they play under the Duke's window. Normally it's their own children who provide the early morning alarm. In the corridor they have a slide, trampoline and climbing frame to keep them amused. When boredom sets in they run into their parent's bedroom where two drawers of toys and puzzles are kept.

The Duke genuinely enjoys his children, taking them for walks in Kensington Gardens and occasionally for a ride up the private royal drive on the handlebars of his motorbike. One day a joy ride nearly turned into tragedy when a delivery van shot out of a side alley and missed the Duke and his son, Alexander, by a few inches.

The Duke took the official pictures of his daughter Lady Rose after her birth and their family album is full of snaps of

Alexander in his hospital incubator. Richard has illustrated three books with his photographs and prefers to give them, rather than cufflinks, as Christmas presents.

Although he enjoys his children's company, when it comes to mealtimes the children are under the eye of their nanny. They are fussy eaters who can go literally for days hardly touching a morsel. Many is the time the Duchess has come back from a weekend at Barnwell and told the nanny: 'See what you can do about feeding them. I can't get them to eat anything.' Fish fingers, beans, hot dogs are their staple fare. They will only eat yoghurt if it is strained (a Danish custom) and if it is pink. It is little wonder that the royal couple have had a procession of nannies through their door.

The Duchess is actively involved in her children's upbringing, driving them to school in her Metro, ferrying them to dance and music classes, and trying if possible to devote every third week to family life rather than royal duties.

The couple make a point of not allowing their children to see them leave by a royal helicopter, although they like them to be at Perks Field to wave to them when they land. Normally they arrive home in time for tea – and a story. The Duke of Gloucester loves sitting on the bed reading endless stories about Asterix the Gaul, church cats and mythical kingdoms of fairies and elves. If the children have behaved themselves, on Friday as a treat they are allowed to eat with their parents in the dining room. Simple food – cottage pie, lemon surprise and chocolate cake – is usually the order of the day.

While the children are fussy eaters, the Duke of Gloucester has just one abiding passion in his life: chocolate. He eats chocolate bars, chocolate puddings and cake – the stickier the better – whenever he can. Afternoon tea for example normally consists of toasted sandwiches and a large chocolate cake. Birgitte is in control of how much he is allowed. When she notices that his waistline is thickening, chocolate cake is off the menu until he loses a few pounds. Like many Danes her own particular weakness is for French soft cheese. She is forever raiding the refrigerator for extra portions. Echoes of her Danish upbringing are also in the fact that she serves children steaming mugs of hot chocolate at afternoon tea parties.

However, like the Wales the couple have simple tastes. Indeed, they make Diana and Charles look positively dissolute in their eating habits. For breakfast the Duke has grapefruit, and toast with a glass of milk, orange juice or water. Richard, a teetotaller, feels that even tea and coffee are bad for the system. (As the Duke dislikes the taste of alcohol, the Duchess chooses the wine for dinner parties. As a result she has become quite an expert.) The Duchess, however, starts the day with cereal and eggs and orders something simple such as cottage pie or fish for lunch. Onions and garlic together with wine sauces are banned from their diet.

So long is the list of 'Do's and Don'ts' that when a new cook starts he receives four pages of closely typed instructions. This attention to detail is reminiscent of Richard's father. In his day he insisted that next to every ashtray there had to lie a cigarette and beside the cigarette a matchbox in a solid silver cover with a match sticking out, in order to save the trouble of opening it. Perhaps this is one reason why his son is such a vociferous anti-smoker; he is patron of ASH (Action for Smoking and Health), even handing out badges to young ladies which say: 'Kiss a non-smoker, taste the difference'.

The relative hardships faced by the modern Gloucesters have been well noted by Princess Alice who rather regrets the passing of the old order. Perhaps she is right. Gone are the days when the previous Duke of Gloucester could watch a log fall from the fire, leave it smouldering on the carpet and then say: 'About time too' when a passing servant removed it when he smelled smoke.

However the Gloucesters still employ a substantial staff, second only to the Prince and Princess of Wales. Besides a cook, nanny and maid they also have a butler from the Irish Hussars, an under butler/valet and two chauffeurs – paid for by the Royal Corps of Transport of which Princess Alice is Colonel-in-Chief.

While the couple are fussy they have few major staff problems. Employees are used to seeing the Duke wandering around with his head in a book, delegating all household decisions to his wife who usually knows exactly what she wants. The only restrictions on staff are those regarding their relations with staff from other royal Houses, particularly that of Prince and Princess Michael of Kent. While the Duchess does not stop staff associating with their opposite numbers in the Michaels' household, fraternization is frowned on. For reasons already mentioned there is little love lost between the two royal couples. Often the Duchess will make deprecating remarks about her royal rival when her photograph appears in the paper.

While Birgitte likes her anonymity she does like to be recognized when she goes out in public. One of the most galling moments came during the wedding of the Prince and Princess of Wales, when the Duchess was leaving Buckingham Palace in an official limousine. As she drove out between the famous wrought-iron gates, the crowd stood there, cameras poised, ready to snap the occupants. When they saw the Duchess no one had a clue who she was and the cameras that were raised expectantly were quickly lowered. Birgitte gritted her teeth grimly, no doubt feeling that duty does not have its just reward. For while uncontroversial, the couple have made a significant contribution to the work of the family firm – even if it has not made front page news.

One of the most upsetting aspects about their concern to keep their children out of the limelight has been the number of letters, ranging from the censorious to the cranky, from members of the public. Because the children have their photographs released rarely, this led to a spare of hate mail to the Duchess making disturbing allegations about her children's physical and mental health.

This mirrors a similar situation when Prince Andrew was small and the Queen deliberately kept him out of the limelight. The result again was hate mail suggesting that the Prince was mentally retarded and rumours that he was kept out of the public gaze because the royal family were ashamed of him. This is the dark side of life for a public figure which is rarely referred to, but is hurtful nonetheless.

In general the Duke and Duchess are content with the balance they have achieved between private family life and public life, especially for the children's sake. 'We are very happy where we are,' says the Duke. 'It's always nice for children to see other children around and they bump into each other when their nannies ferry them to and from school. There are no ghosts here but all the floorboards creak.'

Above all it is a happy home where one is surprisingly close to nature. The Duke says: 'One hears the birds and you look out the window and you can see kites that people fly in Kensington Gardens.'

'When there is a thunderstorm, I look out of my room and I can see a row of white classic urns on the top of the southern façade. If you get the sun shining on that with the black thunder-cloud behind, it can be very dramatic.'

If the Duke has a complaint it is that the apartment is so draughty it puts up their heating bill – the palace has a central boiler and all the residents pay a proportion of the bill.

However Kensington Palace is not as bad as Barnwell, where, even if Princess Alice turns on the heating on Friday, the mansion doesn't warm up until it is time to go home on Sunday. 'We end up being issued with hot water bottles to cuddle', says one member of staff.

Since they moved into the twenty-two room Kensington Palace mansion over a decade ago, the Gloucesters have made a number of decorative changes – although when the Duchess went hunting for fabrics she insisted that nothing should be the same as Princess Michael's. On an expedition with her interior designer, Jimmy Smart, and private secretary, they were joined at one store by the Duke of Gloucester who arrived on his motorbike. Once more the shop assistant did not recognize him, thinking he was an upmarket courier. 'But I've come to see my wife,' he pleaded when he was stopped at the door.

The style of their home is comfortable rather than grand, although the Duchess has retained much of the original Georgian character in her choice of fabrics and colours for the apartment. The armchairs sag about as much as the Duke's corduroy trousers while chintz at the windows and muted prints on the walls give their home a sense of the traditional, of continuity.

As a Grade I listed building, a nail cannot be knocked into the walls without seeking permission. This gave the Duchess a headache when she wanted to make a feature out of a Georgian fireplace in the children's playroom. She wished to use the fireplace interior as shelves. Jim Smart, her eccentric and flamboyant Chelsea designer, had the perfect solution. He suggested that the shelves be installed and that the hinged doors be painted black so that it looked like a fireplace. As a final touch he suggested painting a cat on the door as though it were looking into the dummy fireplace, to create a *trompe-l'oeil* effect.

The Duchess was delighted with his neat solution. On the appointed day Jim arrived in his bright pink cadillac, dressed in his fedora, pink tie and pink socks. He made an unusual spectacle when he presented himself to the duty policeman. 'I've come to do some painting,' he said breezily. 'Oh yes,' replied the policeman suspiciously, 'Who for?' Jim said: 'The Duchess of Gloucester. I've come to paint her cat.' That was all the excuse the officer needed. He grabbed Jim's car keys and refused to let him out of his sight until the Duchess had personally verified his status.

Jim's sense of humour didn't always tickle the Duchess pink. For one room they bought an expensive new carpet which was specially woven for them. It took three months to make and on the way down from the factory to Kensington Palace it was stolen. The Duchess was thunderstruck. The next week Jim called in to see her and said impishly: 'I think I've seen your carpet ma'am.' The Duchess was interested. 'Oh really, where?' she asked. 'On television, on the *Police Five* show,' he quipped. Birgitte was not amused.

Like other members of the royal family, the Gloucesters are avid collectors and love to decorate their home with pieces they have picked up from their travels. The Duchess has a growing collection of lacquered wooden ducks that are rapidly becoming very fashionable – and an investor's item.

Though his flair is largely unknown, the Duke is an eager collector of treasures as disparate as coloured stone eggs, modern turned English boxes and Chinese ceramics, and his side tables at Kensington Palace are ranged with examples of modern British craftsmanship in woods from every part of the world. His eggs are displayed in glass cases to set off the beautiful workmanship and markings of eggs wrought in quartz, malachite, lapis lazuli and even dinosaur bones.

For fun the Duke also has a collection of hats hung on the walls of his study, ranging from those from the Stella Artois tennis tournament to mementoes from a visit to China and Nepal where he went hiking. However the real core of the Duke's life is the stuff of schoolboy fantasy. The first clue is in the entrance hall where two model tanks stand guard, for the Duke is fascinated by military life. His library is filled with books on military history, including every volume on the Falklands War, which he followed avidly. In the evening he will make models of military vehicles, trains and ships, or paint toy soldiers while he listens on his stereo to military music or brass bands. His imagination really runs riot at Barnwell. Here he has set aside one room for his soldiers. They cover the carpet as they take up the exact dispositions of troops during World War I battles. But this schoolboy Shangri-La does not end here. The Duke also has a full scale model railway laid out with signals, trees, stations, and every conceivable detail an enthusiast salivates over.

Just to get him in the mood for the battles to come he spends hours in the evening at Kensington Palace hunched over his television set playing Star Wars video games. More conventionally, at the weekends he shoots on his country estate.

While books, battles and brass bands form a central pillar in his life, the Duke does manage to find time to entertain his friends. The Duke and Duchess have a wide circle of friends from the world of design and their student days at Cambridge. They include aristocrats such as Lord and Lady Camoy, architect friends such as Bernard Hunt, Tom Troubridge and the Prince and Princess of Wales. Prince Charles and the Duke have a mutual interest in architecture and the Prince likes to use his neighbour as a sounding board for new ideas and different perspectives.

For their tenth wedding anniversary in 1982 they held open house, to which they invited all the royal family. On that balmy summer evening the Queen and the rest of the royal family were serenaded until the early hours by a steel band. The highlight of the night was a spectacular firework display.

However the main talking point was why Princess Michael of Kent was the only royal lady to arrive in long evening dress and tiara. The party was voted an outstanding success – but it had been touch and go. It was held at the height of the Falklands War and the cautious Duke took the sensible precaution of insuring the party in case Britain lost. If that had happened their anniversary celebrations would have been cancelled.

Normally the Gloucesters' lives are rather less exciting. Steak dinners in front of the television, the opera at Glyndebourne in the summer, skiing in Klosters in Switzerland during the winter. In the days that the Gloucesters went skiing with bachelor Prince Charles, the Prince would ring the Duke to find out if he had got into shape for the holiday. Charles was most disappointed when the Duke blithely reported that he had been doing a little shooting. 'That's not good enough,' Charles complained.

The Duchess, like many royal ladies, keeps fit with regular tennis at Queen's Club. For a busy lady she does not have the benefit, like Diana, of a hairdresser who comes to Kensington Palace. Instead she visits Riche salon in Hay Hill several times a week, usually in the morning.

She and the Duke always make themselves available for discussions with their private secretary Sir Simon Bland, who lives in a two bedroom flat next door. He will often surprise telephone callers who make a request by saying: 'Hang on a minute, I'll just go and ask the Duke.' He says: 'It's wonderful for us but I don't think they get as much privacy as they deserve.'

In fact privacy is the Gloucesters' watchword – and for very serious reasons. They are acutely conscious that the choice of the title 'Earl of Ulster' for their eldest son has singled him out as an IRA terrorist target. Privately they rather regret giving him the title but there is little they can do about it now, apart from being extra vigilant.

However it was the young Earl himself who caused the Gloucesters the biggest scare of their lives. It happened at the height of the IRA's mainland bombing campaign in the early 1980s. The children were safely in bed, the staff were winding down for the day, and the Gloucesters themselves were sitting watching television. All was peace and quiet when suddenly the door burst open and in rushed a dozen flak-jacketed police waving guns in the air. Some ran upstairs, others into the ground floor rooms. The Duke and Duchess were both shocked and surprised by the eruption of activity. 'What the hell is going on,' demanded the Duke. The police quickly realized that it was a false alarm. The culprit was the Duke's son. He had gone into their bedroom and pressed the panic button on the floor by the bed. (There are several in every royal house.) This had sounded the alarm in the police lodge and a carefully rehearsed plan of action had gone into effect. As the squad of police rather sheepishly left the royal apartment young Alexander was brought downstairs and given a severe ticking off by his father.

In the days before the Prince and Princess of Wales arrived security was remarkably lax – in spite of intense IRA bombing campaigns in the capital. When nannies took their royal charges into the park for a walk they were issued with a police whistle, kept under the blanket. They were instructed to blow for help if someone suspicious followed them. 'It was a stupid idea really,' says one former royal nanny. 'If someone had wanted to kidnap one of the royal children they would have been well away before me blowing the whistle had any effect. All it did was make you very nervous about taking the children for a walk. You saw everyone as a potential kidnapper.'

There have been improvements. These days if a royal nanny does not have a Scotland Yard bodyguard accompanying her she is issued with a walkie-talkie to keep in close contact with the police nerve centre in the palace lodge. The ordinary parks police are also alerted about their presence and keep a watchful eye on their perambulations. Princess Diana has taken the IRA death threats so much to heart that she is only happy if a police back-up car plus a bodyguard and nanny take Prince William or Prince Harry out.

When the IRA bombing campaign was at its height during the late 1970s and early 1980s there was a genuine sense of seige at Kensington Palace. Staff were regularly told to stay inside or only allowed to go out with a police escort. Nerves were further worn when bombs went off in Hyde Park and Regents Park, killing a number of military bandsmen and horseguards.

'No one was allowed out,' recalls one servant. 'It was quite terrifying. The windows and doors rattled with the blast, we all thought it was the end of the world.'

Yet ironically it was an unarmed burglar scaling the wall at Buckingham Palace and not the IRA who forced the biggest shakeup in royal security. When Michael Fagan was discovered on the Queen's bed after chatting to her for twenty five minutes, life at Kensington Palace drastically changed.

Fagan's actions, together with the arrival of the Prince and Princess of Wales, shattered the peaceful village atmosphere of Kensington Palace. Given the ferocity and success of the IRA bombing campaign – for a time London was second only to Beirut as the most dangerous capital in the world – security at Kensington Palace was staggeringly complacent. 'Quite frankly it was a joke,' remembers one former staff member. When the IRA were regularly sending letter bombs through the post one royal private secretary would blithely tell his staff as they were opening the mail 'If you get your hands blown off never mind.'

Royal staff did have their own rather subtle ways of getting their own back. If Princess Michael was being particularly difficult her staff had one sure cure to bring her down a peg or two. They knew that she was particularly jittery about terrorist threats and so when a padded package arrived for her – the telltale sign of a letter bomb – they would not open it themselves. Instead they would put the package, which invariably contained a book from a publisher, on her breakfast tray together with the rest of her morning mail. After about thirty minutes the Princess would phone down from her bedroom saying lamely: 'I haven't got time to open these parcels, can you see to it for me?' The package was duly taken away and an improvised safety test put into effect. A staff member would pick up the padded package, stand at the open door of the spare room and then hurl it against the wall, while promptly shutting the door. If it did not explode, the rather battered book would be given to the by now subdued Princess.

Thankfully these ludicrous measures have been replaced by an electronic scanning machine that tests each item of mail coming into Kensington Palace. However even now some security plans have a certain PJ Wodehouse quality about them. If, in the unlikely event an intruder gets into Windsor Castle, the scheme is to lock all the royal family in their various towers while a search party of police, valets and butlers – no doubt in their silk dressing gowns and armed with brass pokers – will look for the villain.

It was the Jeevesian quality about Kensington Palace which made it such an amiable place to live. The police lodge was an informal meeting point where off duty staff would wander in for a chat. They organized various impromptu parties – Geordie nights where they all drank brown ale or Scottish nights where whisky was the evening's tipple – and everyone had a jolly good time.

One evening it was a godsend that a party was in progress. A patrolling officer spotted an intruder climbing over the fence from millionaire's row and walking over the grass towards the palace apartments. The officer made haste to tackle the man. All of a sudden from beneath his raincoat the man whipped out a huge Samurai sword that glinted wickedly in the moonlight. He stood there in the traditional warrior position, legs half bent, sword vertical above his head, quivering and poised to leap into action. The policeman nearly fainted but recovered sufficiently to make a dash to safety. He ran into the lodge about fifty yards away and raised the alarm.

Shirt-sleeved police and several servants ran out to overpower the intruder. They discovered him standing stock still in exactly the same position. When the man, an obvious crank, was questioned he told his interrogators that he wanted to see Prince Charles. 'You should have written first,' commented one officer drily.

In addition to the annual crop of mentally deranged individuals and drunks, there are also professional thieves who see Kensington Palace as a tempting target. One youth who tried his luck was quickly captured by police. He told them: 'When I come near to Kensington Gardens I thought, Margaret and Snowdon live there so there must be some good gear.' The only phrase missing from this Cockney lad's alleged statement was the phrase: 'It's a fair cop guv, I'll come quiet.'

Perhaps the unluckiest sneak thieves were a pair of likely lads who didn't even realize that Kensington Palace existed. They had just burgled a Kensington hotel and were running across Kensington Gardens with their haul when they noticed the wall running around the royal apartments. Thinking that this was a quick exit on to the Bayswater Road, which runs to the north of the Palace, they threw over their swag and shinned up the wall. By the time they had walked ten yards they had unwelcome company in the shape of half a dozen police officers.

Princess Michael got into trouble with the police herself because of her own cavalier approach to security. When she was preparing for a grand state occasion she always used to take her diamond tiara with her when she went to the hairdresser Hugh Green in Ebury Street. However the police got to hear of this practice and were horrified. Memos were exchanged and the Princess was advised to stop the habit.

It was the same security reasons that prevented the Gloucesters' private secretary from offering the winner of a raffle in his Kent village the chance to spend the night in his Kensington Palace *pied-à-terre*. 'The police felt it might attract undesirables,' he explained when he withdrew the offer.

Such innocent offers are now a thing of the past. Since the Fagan incident, and following the Dellow Report into royal security, all the fun has gone out of guarding the royal family. These days everything is laid down, logged and listed – with spy cameras to watch the watchers. 'It is amazing what one guy climbing over a wall can do,' said one officer ruefully.

There are plans for every eventuality. In time of war the Broad Walk in Kensington Gardens would be converted into an airstrip to fly the royals to safety on board a short-takeoff plane.

While the more professional approach has spoiled the relaxed atmosphere of Kensington Palace, at least the royals can sleep more easily in their beds. Indeed as Buckingham Palace becomes more the royal office block and Kensington Palace the royal home, security will become more important.

The Duke and Duchess of York may decide to move into the apartment formerly occupied by Princess Alice, Countess of Athlone. It is certainly appropriate for their royal rank.

Prince Edward too will not be happy to spend his days at Buckingham Palace. The Palace is a cheerless, cold tomb for all its superficial glamour. There is not one member of the royal family who enjoys living there and the Queen skips town as soon as she can at lunch time on Friday to go to Sandringham or Windsor. The use of Sandringham is increasing so rapidly that it would come as no surprise that as the Queen – now a pensioner – slips into semi-retirement her Norfolk home will be used as the semi-official court.

It was a problem forseen twenty years ago by Labour Minister Richard Crossman. In his diary he noted the Queen's feelings for Sandringham. He observed: 'At lunch she was very relaxed. "At Sandringham," she told me, "I feel a great deal more remote from London than at Balmoral." They all love this place because it was Edward VII's hideout and has become a family hideout where they feel more like ordinary human beings. It struck me that it would be nice if one could arrange for the Queen to commute from Sandringham in future and use Buckingham Palace merely as an office.'

As this trend continues, as the burden of leadership falls more heavily on Prince Charles's shoulders, Kensington Palace will become even more important as the alternative royal court: a centre of artistic, political and intellectual impetus; a meeting point for national and international decision makers, and at the same time a focal point for the various crowned and deposed heads of Europe and the Middle East to keep the skein of royalty from wearing thin; a unique village of competing vanities, aspirations and values, the delight of sociologists who can observe one special privileged group and see how they act when they are not performing on the royal stage. Then, a glimpse into the royal dressing room, with the make-up off, the costume of convention hanging loosely over the red brick wall, may give you the chance to ask the question: 'What is Diana really like?' – and for once get a straight answer.

Bibliography

Alexandra of Yugoslavia, HM Queen *Prince Philip, A Family Portrait* (Cassell, 1973)

Alice, Princess, Duchess of Gloucester *Memoirs* (Collins, 1983)

Aronson, Theo *Grandmama of Europe* (Cassell, 1973)

Barry, Stephen *Royal Secrets* (Villard Books, 1985)

Burnet, Sir Alastair *In Person: The Prince and Princess of Wales* (Independent Television News/Michael O'Mara Books, 1985)

Burnet, Sir Alastair *In Public – In Private: The Prince and Princess of Wales* (Independent Television News/Michael O'Mara Books, 1986)

Crossman, Richard *Diaries of a Cabinet Minister Vol II* (Hamish Hamilton, 1976)

Dean, John *Valet to the Duke of Edinburgh* (Robert Hale, 1954)

Duff, David *The Life Story of HRH Princess Louise* (Stanley Paul, 1940)

Frere, JA *The British Monarchy at Home* (Anthony Gibbs & Phillips, 1963)

Geldof, Bob *Is That It?* (Penguin, 1986)

Hedley, Olwen *Kensington Palace: the State Apartments* (Pitkin, 1976)

Hennessy, James Pope *Queen Mary* (George Allen & Unwin, 1959)

Hough, Richard *Louis and Victoria: the first Mountbattens* (Hutchinson, 1974)

Hudson, Derek *Kensington Palace* (Peter Davies, 1968)

Longford, Elizabeth *Victoria, RI* (Weidenfeld and Nicolson, 1964)

Martin, Ralph *Charles and Diana* (Grafton Books, 1985)

Pearson, John *The Ultimate Family: The Making of the Royal House of Windsor* (Michael Joseph, 1986)

Robertson, Jillian *The Royal Race for the British Crown 1917–19* (Blond and Briggs, 1977)

Russell, Peter *Butler Royal* (Hutchinson, 1962)

Sunday Express *A Week in the Life of the Royal Family* (Weidenfeld and Nicholson, 1983)

Warwick, Christopher *Princess Margaret* (Weidenfeld and Nicholson, 1983)

Whiting, Audrey *The Kents, A Royal Family* (Hutchinson, 1985)

Index

Picture Acknowledgements

Alpha
Camera Press
Arthur Edwards
Tim Graham
London Express News and Features
    Services
Al Lorenz/People Weekly

Julian Parker
Popperfoto
South West News Services
Frank Spooner Pictures
Syndication International
Topham Picture Library